# WAR TRAVEL GUIDE

# GREGOR STEVES

# COPYRIGHT ©

All rights reserved. No part of this publication may be reproduced, distributed, or transmitted in any form or by any means, including photocopying, recording, or other electronic or mechanical methods, without the prior written permission of the publisher, except in the case of brief quotations embodied in critical reviews and certain other noncommercial uses permitted by copyright law.

# DISCLAIMER

The information provided in this travel guide is for general informational purposes only. While every effort has been made to ensure the accuracy of the content, the author and publisher assume no responsibility for errors or omissions, or for any loss or damage resulting from the use of this information. Travelers are advised to check with local authorities, businesses, and resources for the most up-to-date information.

This guide includes recommendations based on the author's personal experiences and opinions. Individual experiences may vary, and readers are encouraged to exercise their own judgment and discretion when planning their travels.

The author and publisher do not endorse or guarantee any specific service, product, or business mentioned in this guide. Any reliance on such information is solely at the reader's responsibility.

All travel involves inherent risks, and readers are advised to take appropriate precautions, including securing travel insurance. The author and publisher shall not be held liable for any injuries, damages, or losses that may occur during travel.

# TABLE OF CONTENT

INTRODUCTION .................................................. 8
    Why Warsaw ................................................ 10
    Unveiling the City's Multifaceted Charm ............... 11

**CHAPTER 1** ..................................................... 15
    A Tapestry of Time: Warsaw's Historical Evolution
    ................................................................. 18
    Modernity Meets Tradition: Warsaw Today .......... 20
    Getting Around: Navigating the City with Ease .... 22

**CHAPTER 2** ..................................................... 24
    The Royal Castle: A ResurrectedSymbol of Polish Heritage ........................................................ 25
    Palace of Culture and Science: A Controversial Icon ................................................................ 28
    The Old Town Market Square: A UNESCO World Heritage Gem .................................................. 32
    Łazienki Park: An Oasis of Greenery and Palaces
    ................................................................. 34
    POLIN Museum of the History of Polish Jews: A Tribute to Resilience ....................................... 38

**CHAPTER 3** ..................................................... 42

Pierogi, Paczki, and More: Discovering Polish Cuisine ............... 43

Milk Bars: A Taste of Authentic Polish Fare ......... 46

Warsaw's Vibrant Food Scene: Restaurants and Cafés .................. 48

Market Delights: Hala Mirowska and Other Culinary Hubs ................ 50

**CHAPTER 4** ............... 52

Chopin's Legacy: Music in Warsaw ..................... 52

The National Museum: Art and ........................... 54

Artifacts of Poland ................................................ 54

Contemporary Art: Galleries and Street ............... 58

Art ....................................................................... 58

Warsaw's Nightlife: Clubs, Bars, and ................... 60

Live Music Venues ............................................... 60

**CHAPTER 5** ............... 62

Planning Your Visit: When to Go and How Long to Stay ................... 62

Accommodations: Hotels, Hostels, and Apartments ................... 65

Money Matters: Currency, Banking, and Tipping . 70

Getting There and Away: Flights, Trains, and Buses ................... 72

Getting Around: Public Transportation and Taxis ....... 76

**CHAPTER 6** ............................................................. **80**

Praga District: Warsaw's Edgy and Creative Side 80

Żoliborz: A Leafy Residential Enclave ................. 82

Mokotów: Parks, Cafes, and Family-Friendly Vibes
............................................................................ 85

Ochota: A Blend of Old and New ....................... 87

**CHAPTER 7** ............................................................. **90**

Neon Muzeum: A Glowing Tribute to Communist-Era Signage ....................... 91

The Warsaw Rising Museum: Stories of Resistance and Heroism......................... 93

Wilanów Palace: A Baroque Masterpiece on the Outskirts............................. 97

The Vistula River: Recreation and Riverfront Views
............................................................................ 99

**CHAPTER 8** ........................................................... **102**

Rooftop Bars: Capture Warsaw's Skyline .......... 103

Old Town Charm: Architectural Photography Tips
.......................................................................... 105

Street Scenes: Documenting Warsaw's Daily Life
.......................................................................... 107

Parks and Gardens: Nature Photography Opportunities ..................................................... 109

## CHAPTER 9 ........................................................... 112

Health and Safety Tips for Travelers ................... 113

Cultural Norms and Etiquette in Warsaw ........... 115

Emergency Contacts and Information ................. 118

## CHAPTER 10 ......................................................... 122

Treblinka Memorial: A Solemn Reminder ........... 122

Żelazowa Wola: Birthplace of Chopin ................. 125

Kampinos National Park: Nature Escape ........... 127

## CHAPTER 11 ......................................................... 130

Your Warsaw Questions Answered .................... 130

## BONUS ................................................................. 134

One Day in Warsaw: The Essentials ................... 134

Three Days in Warsaw: A Deeper Dive .............. 135

One Week in Warsaw: The ................................. 136

Comprehensive Itinerary ..................................... 136

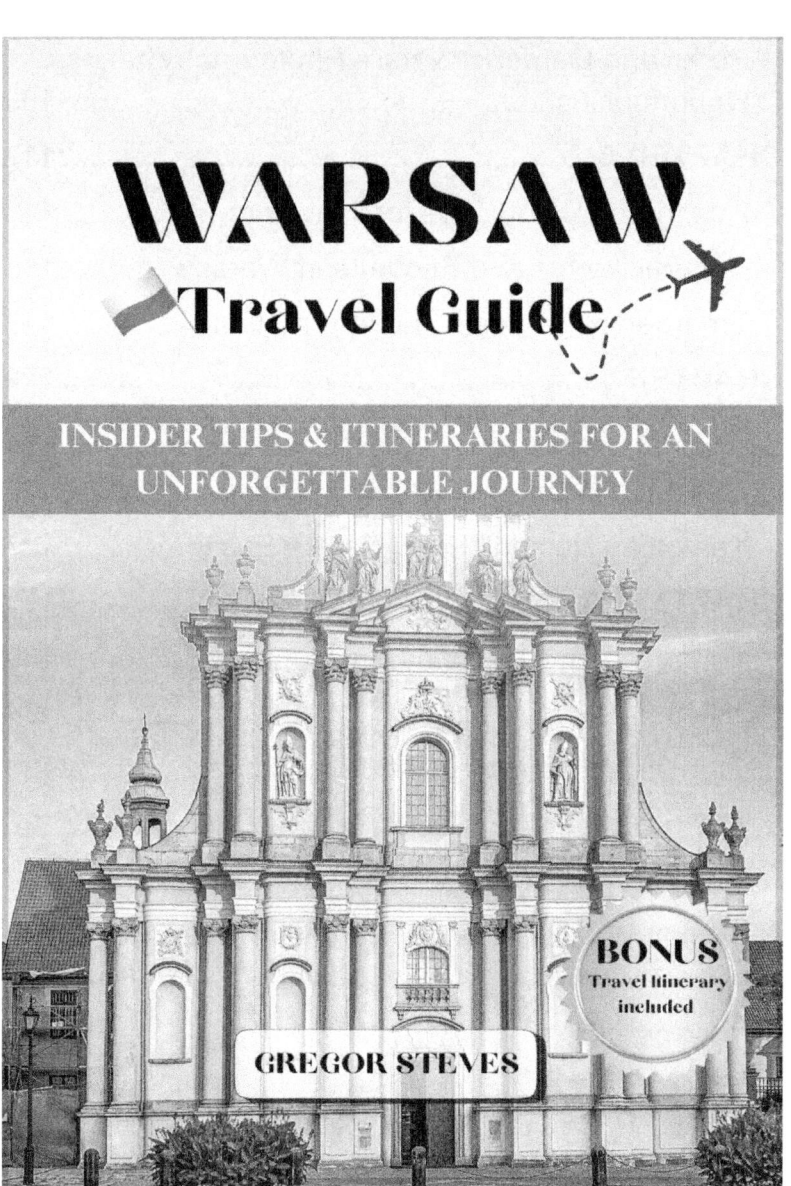

# INTRODUCTION

The Warsaw sun, a warm caress on my face, reflected off the gilded dome of St. Anne's Church. As I wandered through the cobbled streets of the Old Town, rebuilt with love after the ravages of war, I felt a whisper of history on every corner.

My journey led me to the majestic Royal Castle Square, a wide expanse where centuries of Polish monarchs once held court. Sunlight danced on the vibrant facades, each stone whispering tales of resilience and rebirth. I paused by the towering Zygmunt's Column, a bronze sentinel watching over the city, a reminder of Warsaw's enduring spirit.

The city's heart, I discovered, beat strongest in its people. A spirited street performer, his violin weaving a melody of joy and sorrow, drew a crowd of all ages. Families strolled hand-in-hand, laughter mingling with the sweet scent of blooming lilacs. Market vendors, their stalls overflowing with colorful wares, engaged in lively banter with shoppers.

As I delved deeper into Warsaw's embrace, I found remnants of its complex past. The somber POLIN Museum, a testament to the resilience of the Jewish community, shared stories of triumph and tragedy. The imposing Palace of Culture and Science, a gift from Stalin, loomed over the city, a stark reminder of an era of both hardship and progress.

My wanderings continued to the tranquil Łazienki Park, a lush haven where peacocks strutted amidst sculpted gardens. I paused on a bridge, watching swans glide across the shimmering lake, their elegance mirroring the city's own beauty.

In the evening, as the sky transformed into a canvas of vibrant hues, I climbed to the rooftop terrace of a trendy bar. The city spread out before me, a sparkling tapestry of lights and shadows. It was a panorama that revealed Warsaw's layers, from its historic heart to its modern pulse.

Warsaw had captivated me with its blend of old and new, its rich history and vibrant present. It was a city of stories, etched in every cobblestone, every monument, every smile. A city that had risen from the ashes, stronger and more beautiful than ever before. A city I was eager to explore, to understand, to share with the world.

## Why Warsaw

The question echoes with a thousand answers, each as unique as the city itself. Warsaw is a city that wears its history proudly, a living testament to resilience and rebirth. History enthusiasts will find themselves spellbound by the meticulous reconstruction of the Old Town, a UNESCO World Heritage site that emerged from the ashes of World War II. Wander through the cobbled streets, marvel at the architectural details, and imagine the vibrant life that once filled these historic squares.

But Warsaw is more than just its past. It's a city that embraces modernity, pulsating with creative energy and a burgeoning arts scene. Art aficionados will discover a treasure trove of galleries, museums, and street art installations, while music lovers can revel in the city's rich musical heritage, from Chopin concerts to contemporary jazz clubs.

Foodies will find their palates tantalized by Warsaw's culinary landscape. From traditional Polish pierogi and hearty bigos to innovative fusion cuisine and international flavors, the city's dining scene is a feast for the senses. Don't miss the chance to experience the authentic charm of a milk bar, where affordable and delicious Polish classics await.

Nature enthusiasts will find solace in Warsaw's numerous parks and green spaces. Stroll through the meticulously manicured gardens of Łazienki Park, admire the vibrant blooms of the Saxon Garden, or escape the urban hustle and bustle in the serene Kampinos National Park, a haven for hiking, cycling, and wildlife watching.

For those seeking a vibrant nightlife, Warsaw delivers. Trendy bars, pulsating clubs, and live music venues beckon after dark, offering a diverse range of experiences to suit every taste. Whether you're sipping cocktails on a rooftop terrace with panoramic city views or dancing the night away to electronic beats, Warsaw's nightlife won't disappoint.

Warsaw is a city that defies easy categorization. It's a place where history and modernity coexist, where tradition and innovation intertwine. It's a city that invites you to explore its many facets, to discover its hidden gems, and to create your own unique adventure. So, why Warsaw? Because it's a city that will leave an indelible mark on your heart and soul.

## Unveiling the City's Multifaceted Charm

Warsaw, a city of captivating contrasts, beckons with a multifaceted charm that unfolds at every turn. Within its vibrant tapestry, you'll discover a harmonious blend of historical grandeur and contemporary dynamism, a testament to its resilience and unwavering spirit.

Delve into the heart of the city and find yourself immersed in the Old Town's enchanting embrace. Meander through narrow lanes, where colorful facades adorned with intricate details tell tales of bygone eras. The majestic Royal Castle, a symbol of Polish heritage, stands proudly, its reconstructed walls whispering stories of kings and queens. Nearby, the Old Town Market Square, a UNESCO World Heritage site, buzzes with life, its charming cafes and bustling market stalls inviting you to linger.

Venture beyond the historic center and witness Warsaw's modern metamorphosis. The skyline is punctuated by sleek skyscrapers, showcasing the city's ambition and progress. The Palace of Culture and Science, a controversial icon, towers over the cityscape, offering panoramic views from its observation deck. Stroll along the revitalized riverfront, where trendy bars and restaurants offer a taste of Warsaw's vibrant nightlife.

Warsaw's cultural scene is a symphony of creativity and expression. Immerse yourself in the world of Chopin at the Fryderyk Chopin Museum, or catch a performance at the National Philharmonic. Explore the National Museum's vast collection of art and artifacts, or discover cutting-edge contemporary works at the Ujazdowski Castle Centre for Contemporary Art.

For those seeking culinary adventures, Warsaw is a paradise of flavors. Indulge in traditional Polish cuisine at cozy milk bars, where hearty pierogi and savory bigos satisfy both body and soul. Explore the city's thriving restaurant scene, where innovative chefs fuse local ingredients with global influences. And don't miss the chance to wander through the colorful stalls of Hala Mirowska, a bustling market overflowing with fresh produce, local specialties, and international treats.

Nature lovers will find solace in Warsaw's verdant parks and gardens. Stroll through the meticulously manicured grounds of Łazienki Park, where peacocks strut amidst tranquil lakes and elegant palaces. Discover the Saxon Garden's hidden corners, or escape to the sprawling wilderness of Kampinos National Park, a haven for hiking, biking, and wildlife watching.

Whether you're a history buff, an art enthusiast, a foodie, or a nature lover, Warsaw has something to ignite your passion. It's a city that embraces its past while looking towards the future, a place where the old and new converge in a harmonious symphony of experiences. Let Warsaw's multifaceted charm captivate your senses and leave you with lasting memories of a city that truly has it all.

# WARSAW

## HOW TO USE

1. Download a QR Code Reader App.
2. Open the QR Code Reader App.
3. Position the QR Code in the Frame.
4. Scan the QR Code.
5. Access the maps.

# CHAPTER 1

## WARSAW'S STORY

Warsaw, a city steeped in history, bears witness to centuries of triumphs and tribulations. Its story is a testament to the enduring spirit of its people, their unwavering determination to rebuild and thrive in the face of adversity. From its medieval origins to its pivotal role in World War II and its subsequent rebirth, Warsaw's journey is a captivating saga of resilience, innovation, and cultural richness.

The city's roots trace back to the 13th century, when a small settlement emerged on the banks of the Vistula River. Over the centuries, Warsaw grew in prominence, becoming the capital of Poland in the 16th century and a thriving center of trade, culture, and politics. Its architectural landscape blossomed, adorned with majestic palaces, elegant churches, and bustling market squares.

However, Warsaw's path was not without its challenges. The city endured numerous invasions, occupations, and devastating fires, each leaving its mark on the urban fabric. But through it all, Warsaw's spirit remained unbroken, its people rebuilding their beloved city time and again.

The darkest chapter in Warsaw's history unfolded during World War II. The city was subjected to unimaginable destruction, with nearly 85% of its buildings reduced to rubble. The Warsaw Uprising of 1944, a heroic but ultimately tragic act of resistance, further devastated the city. Yet, from the ashes of war, a remarkable transformation began.

With unwavering determination, Warsaw's citizens embarked on a monumental reconstruction effort. Drawing inspiration from historical documents and paintings, they painstakingly rebuilt their cherished landmarks, restoring the Old Town to its former glory. This remarkable feat earned Warsaw the UNESCO World Heritage designation, a testament to the city's resilience and dedication to preserving its cultural heritage.

Today, Warsaw stands as a vibrant metropolis, a testament to the power of human spirit and the ability to overcome adversity. Its streets buzz with life, its cultural scene thrives, and its economy flourishes. The city's architecture reflects its diverse past, from medieval remnants to socialist-era structures and modern skyscrapers.

# A Tapestry of Time: Warsaw's Historical Evolution

A city forged by time, Warsaw's historical evolution is a captivating narrative of resilience, transformation, and cultural richness. Its story begins in the 13th century, when a modest settlement took root on the banks of the Vistula River. This humble beginning laid the foundation for a city that would rise to become the capital of Poland and a vibrant center of trade, culture, and political power.

The medieval era saw Warsaw flourish as a bustling hub, its streets teeming with merchants, artisans, and scholars. The city's skyline was adorned with majestic palaces, ornate churches, and lively market squares. The Royal Castle, a symbol of Polish sovereignty, emerged as a focal point of power and prestige.

In the 17th century, Warsaw faced a series of challenges, including invasions, occupations, and devastating fires. However, each setback only fueled the city's determination to rebuild and thrive. The 18th century witnessed a cultural renaissance, with the establishment of the University of Warsaw and the emergence of a vibrant intellectual and artistic scene.

The 19th century brought further upheaval, as Poland was partitioned and Warsaw found itself under foreign rule. Yet, the city's spirit remained unbroken. The spirit of independence and national identity continued to thrive, culminating in the restoration of Poland's sovereignty after World War I.

The most harrowing chapter in Warsaw's history unfolded during World War II. The city was systematically destroyed by Nazi Germany, its buildings reduced to rubble and its population decimated. The Warsaw Uprising of 1944, a heroic act of resistance against Nazi occupation, further devastated the city.

In the aftermath of the war, Warsaw faced the daunting task of rebuilding from the ashes. With unwavering determination, its citizens embarked on a remarkable reconstruction effort. Guided by historical records and photographs, they meticulously restored the Old Town, recreating its architectural treasures and cultural landmarks. This extraordinary feat earned Warsaw the UNESCO World Heritage designation, a testament to the city's resilience and unwavering commitment to preserving its past.

Today, Warsaw stands as a thriving metropolis, a testament to the power of human spirit and the ability to overcome adversity. Its streets buzz with life, its cultural scene flourishes, and its economy thrives. The city's architecture reflects its diverse past, from medieval remnants and Baroque palaces to socialist-era structures and modern skyscrapers.

## Modernity Meets Tradition: Warsaw Today

Today, Warsaw pulsates with a dynamic energy, a harmonious fusion of its historical legacy and contemporary aspirations. The city's skyline, a striking blend of reconstructed landmarks and modern architectural marvels, reflects this unique interplay between past and present. While the meticulously restored Old Town whispers tales of centuries gone by, gleaming skyscrapers like the Warsaw Spire and the Q22 building stand as symbols of the city's ambition and progress.

Amidst this architectural tapestry, Warsaw's cultural scene thrives, showcasing a vibrant blend of tradition and innovation. Art enthusiasts will find themselves enthralled by the city's numerous galleries, exhibiting works by both renowned Polish masters and emerging contemporary artists. The Zachęta National Gallery of Art and the Ujazdowski Castle Centre for Contemporary Art are just two examples of the city's thriving artistic landscape.

Beyond the traditional gallery walls, Warsaw's streets themselves have become a canvas for creative expression. Vibrant murals and street art installations adorn building facades, adding a splash of color and personality to the urban landscape. The Praga district, once a gritty industrial area, has transformed into a hub of artistic energy, attracting creatives from all walks of life.

Warsaw's musical heritage, deeply rooted in the works of Frédéric Chopin, continues to resonate throughout the city. The annual Chopin Piano Competition draws talented musicians from around the world, while numerous concert halls and venues host performances that celebrate both classical and contemporary music.

But Warsaw's cultural scene extends far beyond music and art. The city's theaters offer a diverse range of productions, from classic Polish plays to cutting-edge experimental performances. The National Theatre, with its opulent interior and rich history, is a cultural landmark in its own right.

As the sun sets, Warsaw's urban life takes on a new dimension. Trendy bars and restaurants, nestled in revitalized neighborhoods and along the picturesque riverfront, come alive with the sounds of laughter, clinking glasses, and lively conversation. Whether you're seeking a cozy wine bar, a bustling pub, or a rooftop terrace with panoramic views, Warsaw's nightlife caters to every taste and preference.

# Getting Around: Navigating the City with Ease

Navigating Warsaw is a breeze, thanks to its well-developed transportation network and user-friendly layout. Whether you prefer to explore on foot, hop on public transport, hail a taxi, or cycle through the city's scenic routes, getting around is both convenient and enjoyable.

**PUBLIC TRANSPORTATION:**
Warsaw boasts an extensive public transportation system, comprising buses, trams, metro lines, and suburban trains. The metro, with its two lines crisscrossing the city, is a fast and efficient way to reach major attractions and districts. Trams and buses offer a more scenic journey, allowing you to soak in the city's sights and sounds as you travel.

To use public transport, you'll need a valid ticket, which can be purchased at ticket machines located at most stops and stations, or through mobile apps like Jakdojade or mPay. Consider purchasing a multi-day pass if you plan on using public transport frequently.

## TAXIS:
Taxis are readily available throughout Warsaw, and can be hailed on the street or booked through apps like Uber or Bolt. Be sure to choose licensed taxis with visible meters to avoid any unpleasant surprises.

## BIKE RENTALS:
Warsaw is a cyclist-friendly city, with numerous bike paths and rental stations scattered throughout. Several bike-sharing programs, such as Veturilo, offer convenient and affordable options for exploring the city on two wheels. Cycling is a great way to cover more ground while enjoying the fresh air and scenic views.

## WALKING:
Warsaw's compact city center is easily navigable on foot, and many of its top attractions are within walking distance of each other. Lace up your walking shoes and embark on a leisurely stroll through the Old Town's charming streets, or follow the scenic Vistula River path for picturesque views of the city.

## NAVIGATING THE CITY:
Warsaw's layout is relatively straightforward, with the Vistula River dividing the city into two main sections. The Old Town and many historical landmarks are located on the left bank, while the modern city center and business districts are on the right bank.

# CHAPTER 2

## WARSAW'S ICONIC LANDMARKS

Warsaw's skyline, a captivating blend of historic grandeur and modern innovation, is punctuated by iconic landmarks that beckon exploration. Each structure, steeped in history and architectural significance, tells a unique story of the city's past, present, and future. From the majestic Royal Castle to the towering Palace of Culture and Science, these landmarks stand as testaments to Warsaw's resilience, creativity, and enduring spirit.

The Royal Castle, a symbol of Polish heritage and national pride, invites you to step back in time and explore the opulent chambers where monarchs once held court. The Palace of Culture and Science, a controversial yet iconic structure, offers panoramic views of the city from its observation deck, while the Old Town Market Square, a UNESCO World Heritage site, enchants with its colorful facades, lively atmosphere, and charming cafes.

Beyond these well-known landmarks, Warsaw boasts hidden treasures waiting to be discovered. The tranquil Łazienki Park, a verdant oasis in the heart of the city, is home to elegant palaces, picturesque lakes, and enchanting gardens. The POLIN Museum of the History of Polish Jews, a poignant tribute to the resilience of the Jewish community, offers a profound and moving experience.

## The Royal Castle: A Resurrected Symbol of Polish Heritage

The Royal Castle stands as a majestic testament to the unwavering spirit of the Polish people. Once the seat of power for Polish monarchs, this architectural gem was tragically reduced to rubble during World War II. Yet, like the mythical bird, it has been meticulously resurrected, brick by brick, to reclaim its place as a symbol of national pride and resilience.

**A GLIMPSE INTO ROYAL LIFE:**
Step inside the castle's walls and be transported back in time to an era of regal splendor. Wander through the opulent royal apartments, adorned with intricate stuccowork, gilded ceilings, and ornate furnishings. Admire the vast collection of paintings, sculptures, and tapestries that grace the walls, showcasing the artistic and cultural heritage of Poland.

The castle's grand halls, once echoing with the footsteps of kings and queens, now invite visitors to relive the grandeur of bygone eras. The Ballroom, with its shimmering chandeliers and polished marble floors, conjures up images of lavish balls and royal ceremonies. The Throne Room, adorned with regal symbols and rich tapestries, offers a glimpse into the seat of power where monarchs once made decisions that shaped the nation's destiny.

**A TESTAMENT TO RESILIENCE:**
The Royal Castle's destruction during World War II was a devastating blow to the Polish people. Yet, it also fueled their determination to rebuild their beloved landmark. The meticulous reconstruction, based on historical documents, paintings, and photographs, is a testament to the unwavering spirit and dedication of the Polish nation.

Today, the Royal Castle stands as a symbol of hope and resilience, a reminder that even in the face of unimaginable destruction, the human spirit can triumph. It is a place where history comes alive, where the past and present intertwine, and where visitors can experience the grandeur of a bygone era while celebrating the indomitable spirit of a nation.

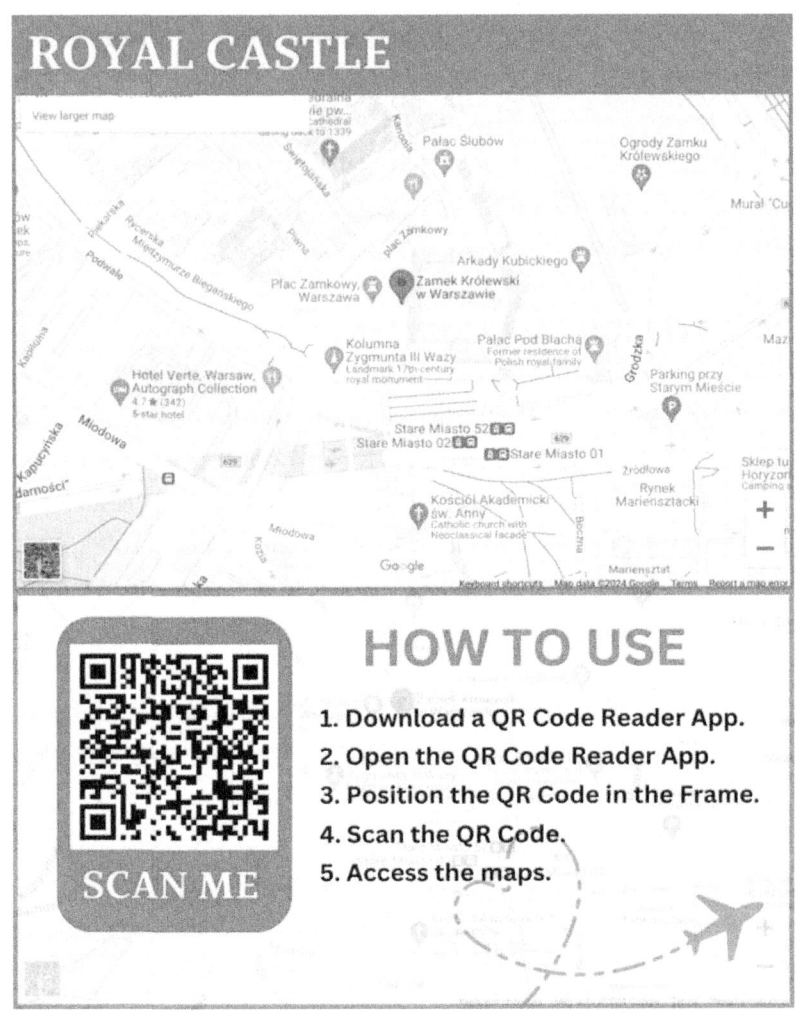

**VISITOR INFORMATION:**
- **Address:** Plac Zamkowy 4, 00-277 Warszawa
- **Contact:** +48 22 355 51 70

- **Hours:** This varies Check the official website for the most up-to-date information.
- **Admission:** Tickets can be purchased online or at the castle's ticket office.
- **Guided Tours:** Available in various languages.
- **Accessibility:** The castle is not really accessible for visitors with disabilities.

**TIPS FOR VISITORS:**
- **Allocate ample time:** Allow at least 2-3 hours to fully explore the castle and its grounds.
- **Bring a camera:** The castle offers numerous photo opportunities.
- **Check for special events:** The castle often hosts concerts, exhibitions, and other cultural events.
- **Visit the Kubicki Arcades:** Located beneath the castle, these arcades house shops, cafes, and restaurants.

# Palace of Culture and Science: A Controversial Icon

A towering testament to a complex past, the Palace of Culture and Science (Pałac Kultury i Nauki) dominates Warsaw's skyline with its imposing presence. This colossal structure, a "gift" from Stalin to the Polish people, has long been a source of both fascination and controversy. Its Socialist Realist architecture, with its soaring spires and ornate details, evokes a bygone era of political ideology and cultural influence.

Love it or loathe it, the Palace of Culture and Science is an undeniable symbol of Warsaw. Its imposing silhouette has become an integral part of the city's identity, a constant reminder of its turbulent past and its unwavering spirit.

Step inside this architectural behemoth and discover a world of diverse activities and cultural offerings. The Palace houses a multitude of museums, including the Museum of Evolution, the Museum of Technology, and the Museum of Warsaw. Its theaters host a variety of performances, from classical concerts to contemporary plays. The Palace also boasts a cinema, a swimming pool, and even a university.

For many, the Palace of Culture and Science represents a dark chapter in Polish history, a symbol of Soviet domination and repression. However, for others, it's a reminder of resilience and the ability to repurpose a controversial landmark for cultural and educational purposes. Regardless of your perspective, the Palace of Culture and Science is a must-see for any visitor to Warsaw. Its complex history, architectural grandeur, and diverse offerings make it a fascinating and thought-provoking destination.

**VISITOR INFORMATION:**
- **Address:** Plac Defilad 1, 00-901 Warszawa
- **Contact:** +48 22 656 76 00
- **Hours:** This varies. Check the official website for the most up-to-date information.
- **Admission:** Tickets can be purchased online or at the Palace's ticket office.
- **Guided Tours:** Available in various languages.
- **Accessibility:** The Palace is partially accessible for visitors with disabilities.

**TIPS FOR VISITORS:**
- **Visit the viewing terrace:** Located on the 30th floor, it offers stunning panoramic views of Warsaw.
- **Explore the museums:** The Palace houses a variety of museums covering different topics.
- **Catch a performance:** Check the schedule for concerts, plays, and other events.
- **Take a guided tour:** Learn about the Palace's history and architecture.
- **Visit the surrounding area:** The Palace is located in the heart of Warsaw, close to other attractions.

# The Old Town Market Square: A UNESCO World Heritage Gem

A vibrant heart pulsates in the center of Warsaw, where the Old Town Market Square (Rynek Starego Miasta) unfolds as a UNESCO World Heritage gem. A kaleidoscope of colors greets you as you step into this historic square, its meticulously reconstructed facades radiating a timeless charm. Each building, a testament to meticulous restoration efforts, whispers stories of centuries past, while the lively atmosphere buzzes with the energy of modern-day Warsaw.

Cobblestone streets wind their way through the square, inviting leisurely strolls and exploration. Pause at a charming cafe to savor a steaming cup of coffee or indulge in a traditional Polish pastry as you watch the world go by. The iconic Mermaid statue, a symbol of Warsaw, stands proudly in the center, a reminder of the city's mythical origins and enduring spirit.

The Old Town Market Square is not just a historical relic; it's a living, breathing testament to the city's vibrant spirit. Street musicians fill the air with melodies, while artists showcase their creations, adding to the lively ambiance. On warm summer evenings, the square transforms into an alfresco dining hub, with tables spilling out onto the cobblestones, inviting locals and visitors alike to enjoy delicious meals under the stars.

As you wander through the square, you'll discover hidden alleyways, charming boutiques, and historical landmarks. The Museum of Warsaw, housed in a series of meticulously restored townhouses, offers a fascinating glimpse into the city's past. The Barbican, a medieval defensive wall, stands as a reminder of Warsaw's turbulent history.

The Old Town Market Square is more than just a tourist attraction; it's a cherished gathering place for locals, a social hub where friends meet, families stroll, and celebrations unfold. It's a testament to the enduring spirit of Warsaw, a city that has risen from the ashes to reclaim its place as a vibrant and captivating destination.

**VISITOR INFORMATION:**
- **Address:** Rynek Starego Miasta, 00-272 Warszawa
- **Contact:** N/A (Public square)
- **Hours:** Open 24 hours
- **Admission:** Free
- **Guided Tours:** Available through various tour operators

- **Accessibility:** The square is accessible, but some of the surrounding streets are cobblestoned.

**TIPS FOR VISITORS:**
- **Enjoy the atmosphere:** Take your time to soak in the ambiance and people-watch.
- **Try the local cuisine:** Sample traditional Polish dishes at one of the many restaurants or cafes.
- **Browse the shops:** The square is surrounded by shops selling souvenirs, crafts, and local products.
- **Attend a cultural event:** Check the schedule for concerts, festivals, and other events.
- **Visit the Museum of Warsaw:** Learn about the city's history and culture.

## Łazienki Park: An Oasis of Greenery and Palaces

An emerald oasis in the heart of Warsaw, Łazienki Park unfurls as a haven of tranquility and timeless elegance. Sunlight filters through the leaves of ancient trees, casting dappled shadows on winding paths that beckon you deeper into this urban sanctuary. The air is filled with the sweet scent of blooming flowers, the gentle rustling of leaves, and the melodic songs of birds.

As you wander through the park's meticulously manicured gardens, you'll discover a harmonious blend of nature and architecture. The Palace on the Isle, a neoclassical gem perched on a tranquil lake, reflects the serene beauty of its surroundings. Its ornate facade, adorned with statues and reliefs, invites you to step inside and explore its opulent interiors.

Nearby, the Myślewicki Palace, a charming summer residence for Polish royalty, exudes a more intimate charm. Its cozy rooms, decorated with period furnishings and artwork, offer a glimpse into the private lives of the past. Stroll through the palace's gardens, where geometric flower beds, sculpted hedges, and trickling fountains create a scene straight out of a fairytale.

The park's open-air theater, nestled among lush greenery, hosts concerts and performances during the warmer months, adding a touch of cultural vibrancy to the tranquil atmosphere. A stroll along the lake's edge reveals picturesque bridges, statues of renowned Polish figures, and graceful swans gliding across the water.

Łazienki Park is more than just a scenic escape; it's a cherished recreational space and a cultural landmark. Locals and tourists alike flock here to relax, unwind, and soak in the beauty of nature. Joggers and cyclists traverse its paths, while families picnic on the lawns and children frolic in the playgrounds. In the evenings, the park transforms into a romantic haven, with couples strolling hand-in-hand under the soft glow of lanterns. Whether you're seeking a peaceful retreat, a cultural immersion, or simply a place to soak up the sun, Łazienki Park offers an enchanting experience that will leave you feeling refreshed and inspired.

**VISITOR INFORMATION:**
- **Address:** Agrykoli 1, 00-460 Warszawa
- **Contact:** +48 22 506 00 10
- **Hours:** Open daily, hours vary by season. Check the official website for the most up-to-date information.
- **Admission:** Free
- **Guided Tours:** Available through various tour operators.
- **Accessibility:** The park is mostly accessible, with some paved paths and ramps.

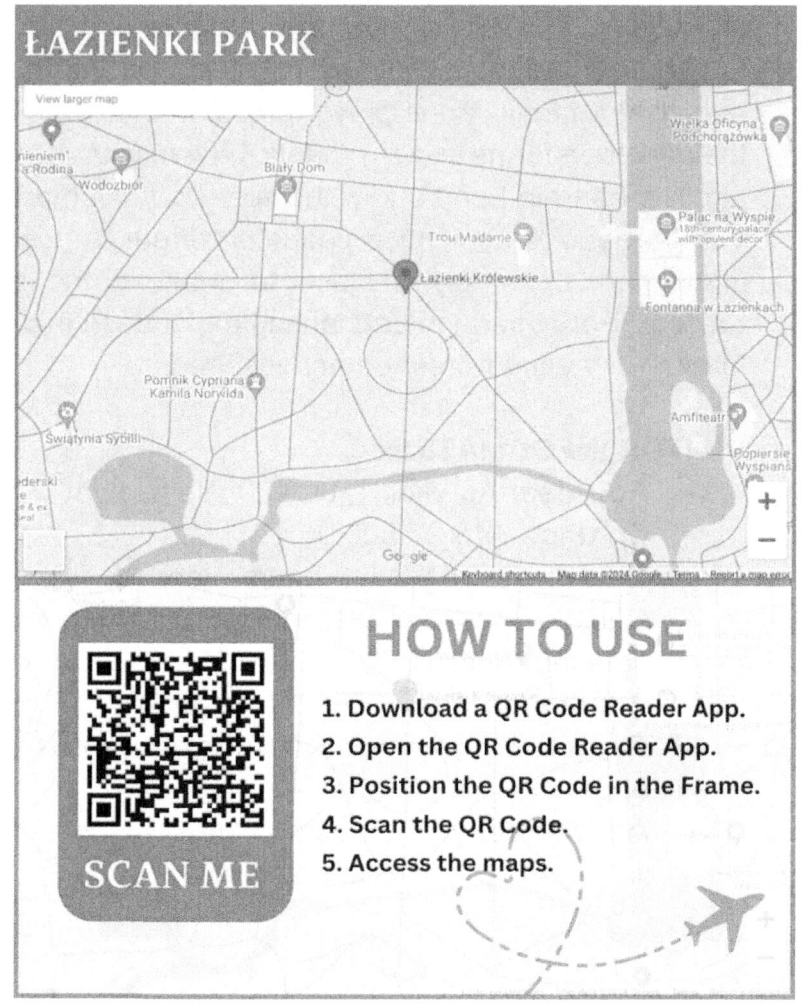

**TIPS FOR VISITORS:**
- **Pack a picnic:** Enjoy a leisurely lunch amidst the park's scenic beauty.

- **Rent a boat:** Paddle around the lake and admire the Palace on the Isle from a different perspective.
- **Attend a concert or performance:** Check the schedule for cultural events at the open-air theater.
- **Visit the Royal Gallery of Sculpture:** Admire a collection of sculptures by renowned Polish artists.
- **Take your time:** Allow ample time to explore the park's many attractions and hidden corners.

# POLIN Museum of the History of Polish Jews: A Tribute to Resilience

A beacon of remembrance and understanding, the POLIN Museum of the History of Polish Jews stands as a testament to a thousand years of shared heritage. Located on the site of the former Warsaw Ghetto, this award-winning institution delves deep into the vibrant tapestry of Jewish life in Poland, from its medieval origins to the present day.

Through immersive exhibits, personal stories, and interactive displays, the POLIN Museum paints a vivid picture of Jewish contributions to Polish culture, science, art, and society. Visitors are invited to walk through meticulously recreated environments, from bustling market squares to humble homes, gaining a deeper understanding of Jewish life in Poland across the centuries.

The museum's architecture is a testament to its mission of openness and dialogue. Its striking glass facade allows natural light to flood the interior, symbolizing transparency and the desire to shed light on a complex and often painful history. The building's design seamlessly blends contemporary aesthetics with elements that evoke the rich heritage of Polish Jewish culture.

The POLIN Museum's impact extends far beyond its exhibits. Its educational programs, lectures, workshops, and cultural events foster dialogue and promote understanding between different communities. By confronting difficult truths and celebrating shared experiences, the museum strives to create a space where everyone feels welcome and valued.

A visit to the POLIN Museum is not just a journey through history; it's an invitation to reflect on the past, engage with the present, and envision a future built on tolerance, empathy, and mutual respect. It's a place where the stories of the Jewish community in Poland are honored, remembered, and shared with the world.

**VISITOR INFORMATION:**
- **Address:** Anielewicza 6, 00-157 Warszawa
- **Contact:** +48 22 471 04 00

- **Hours:** It varies. Check the official website for the most up-to-date information.
- **Admission:** Tickets are available for purchase both online and in the museum's ticket office.
- **Guided Tours:** Available in various languages.
- **Accessibility:** The museum is completely accessible to people with impairments.

**TIPS FOR VISITORS:**
- **Allocate ample time:** Allow at least 3-4 hours to fully explore the museum's exhibits.
- **Visit the core exhibition:** This immersive exhibition tells the story of Polish Jews from the Middle Ages to the present day.
- **Participate in a guided tour:** Gain deeper insights into the museum's collections and themes.
- **Check for temporary exhibitions:** The museum often hosts special exhibitions on various topics related to Jewish history and culture.
- **Visit the Resource Center:** Access a wealth of information and resources on Polish Jewish history and culture.

# CHAPTER 3

## TASTE OF WARSAW

In Warsaw, the aroma of tradition mingles with the zest of innovation, creating a culinary scene that's as diverse and dynamic as the city itself. From hearty peasant fare to elegant Michelin-starred creations, Warsaw's culinary landscape reflects a rich tapestry of flavors, ingredients, and cultural influences.

Embark on a gastronomic adventure and discover the essence of Polish cuisine, where time-honored recipes are passed down through generations, preserving the flavors of the past. Savor the comforting warmth of pierogi, delicate dumplings filled with savory or sweet fillings, or indulge in the crispy sweetness of paczki, a beloved Polish doughnut.

Venture beyond tradition and explore Warsaw's vibrant food scene, where talented chefs are pushing boundaries and reimagining classic dishes with a modern twist. Delight in the innovative flavors of fusion cuisine, where Polish ingredients meet global influences, creating culinary masterpieces that tantalize the taste buds.

Whether you're a seasoned foodie or simply seeking a delicious meal, Warsaw's culinary scene has something to satisfy every craving. From cozy milk bars serving up affordable Polish classics to upscale restaurants showcasing the finest in modern gastronomy, the city's diverse dining options are sure to leave you wanting more.

So, come hungry and let Warsaw's culinary symphony awaken your senses. Discover the unique flavors, traditional dishes, and modern culinary innovations that make this city a true gastronomic destination.

# Pierogi, Paczki, and More: Discovering Polish Cuisine

A culinary journey through Poland is a delightful exploration of flavors, traditions, and regional specialties. From hearty peasant fare to elegant delicacies, Polish cuisine boasts a rich tapestry of dishes that tantalize the taste buds and nourish the soul.

**PIEROGI: A NATIONAL TREASURE**

No culinary adventure in Poland would be complete without savoring the national treasure: pierogi. These delicate dumplings, often lovingly handcrafted, are a testament to Polish culinary ingenuity. From savory fillings like potatoes and cheese (pierogi ruskie) or meat (pierogi z mięsem) to sweet variations bursting with fruits or sweetened farmer's cheese, pierogi cater to every palate. Their versatility and widespread popularity have solidified their status as a beloved staple of Polish cuisine.

## PACZKI: A SWEET INDULGENCE

Indulge your sweet tooth with paczki, a delectable Polish doughnut that holds a special place in the hearts (and stomachs) of locals. Traditionally enjoyed on Fat Thursday, the last Thursday before Lent, these fluffy pastries are filled with a variety of sweet treats, including rose petal jam, plum jam, and Bavarian cream. The irresistible aroma of freshly fried paczki fills the air during carnival season, beckoning all to partake in this delightful indulgence.

## BIGOS: A HEARTY HUNTER'S STEW

For a taste of rustic Polish flavors, delve into a bowl of bigos, a hearty hunter's stew that warms both body and soul. This slow-cooked dish combines a medley of ingredients, including sauerkraut, various meats (often pork, beef, and sausage), dried mushrooms, and a blend of spices. Its complex flavors and rich aroma make it a beloved comfort food, especially during the colder months.

## GOŁĄBKI: STUFFED CABBAGE LEAVES

Embark on a culinary journey to the heart of Polish home cooking with gołąbki, a traditional dish of tender cabbage leaves stuffed with a flavorful mixture of rice, minced meat, and herbs. Baked to perfection in a savory tomato sauce, gołąbki is a testament to the resourcefulness and culinary creativity of Polish cooks. This dish is often served during special occasions and family gatherings, symbolizing warmth, togetherness, and a shared appreciation for traditional flavors.

## ŻUREK: SOUR RYE SOUP

Awaken your taste buds with żurek, a tangy and flavorful sour rye soup that's a true Polish classic. Made from fermented rye flour, this soup is a unique culinary experience. Often served in a bread bowl and garnished with boiled eggs, sausage, and herbs, żurek is a hearty and satisfying dish that's sure to leave a lasting impression.

These are just a few examples of the culinary treasures that await you in Warsaw. From traditional recipes passed down through generations to innovative culinary creations, the city's food scene is a reflection of its rich history, cultural diversity, and unwavering spirit

# Milk Bars: A Taste of Authentic Polish Fare

Step back in time and into a culinary haven where tradition meets affordability. Welcome to the world of milk bars (bar mleczny), a cherished Polish institution that offers a taste of authentic Polish fare without breaking the bank. These unpretentious eateries, with their no-frills decor and communal tables, are a window into Poland's past and a testament to its enduring love for simple, hearty cuisine.

Born out of necessity during the post-war communist era, milk bars were initially subsidized by the government to provide affordable meals for the working class. While the subsidies have largely disappeared, these charming establishments continue to thrive, drawing in a diverse crowd of students, pensioners, and budget-conscious diners seeking a taste of home-cooked goodness.

The menu at a milk bar is a culinary journey through Poland's traditional flavors. Expect to find a variety of pierogi, from the classic potato and cheese (pierogi ruskie) to more adventurous fillings like sauerkraut and mushrooms. Hearty soups, such as tomato soup (zupa pomidorowa) or dill pickle soup (zupa ogórkowa), warm the soul on chilly days. Meat lovers can savor flavorful dishes like kotlet schabowy (breaded pork cutlet) or gołąbki (stuffed cabbage leaves), while vegetarians can delight in pierogi with lentils or spinach and cheese filling.

Milk bars are not just about the food; they're about the experience. The bustling atmosphere, communal seating, and friendly staff create a sense of community and shared enjoyment. The quick service and affordable prices make it easy to grab a delicious meal on the go, while the generous portions ensure you won't leave hungry.

Whether you're a curious traveler seeking an authentic culinary experience or a local looking for a taste of home, milk bars offer a unique window into Polish culture and cuisine. Embrace the unpretentious charm, savor the traditional flavors, and discover why milk bars hold a special place in the hearts of Warsaw's residents.

**PRACTICAL TIPS FOR VISITING MILK BARS:**
- **Don't be afraid to ask for help:** Menus are often in Polish, so don't hesitate to ask the staff for recommendations or translations.
- **Learn a few key phrases:** Knowing a few basic Polish phrases, like "dzień dobry" (good morning/day) and "dziękuję" (thank you), will go

a long way in showing your appreciation for the local culture.
- **Be prepared to share a table:** Communal seating is common in milk bars, so embrace the opportunity to chat with locals and fellow travelers.
- **Order at the counter:** Most milk bars have a self-service system, so you'll need to order and pay at the counter before finding a seat.
- **Try the kompot:** This refreshing fruit-based drink is a popular accompaniment to milk bar meals.

# Warsaw's Vibrant Food Scene: Restaurants and Cafés

Warsaw's culinary scene is a dynamic tapestry of flavors and experiences, reflecting the city's cosmopolitan spirit and innovative culinary talent. From Michelin-starred elegance to cozy cafes tucked away in hidden corners, the city's diverse range of restaurants and eateries caters to every palate and budget.

For a taste of modern Polish cuisine, venture to the upscale restaurants that are reimagining traditional dishes with a contemporary flair. **Atelier Amaro**, the first Polish restaurant to earn a Michelin star, showcases innovative tasting menus that highlight seasonal ingredients and local flavors. **Belvedere Restaurant**, located in the historic Łazienki Park, offers a refined dining experience with its elegant setting and sophisticated menu.

For a more casual yet equally delicious experience, explore the city's vibrant neighborhoods, where cozy cafes and bistros serve up comforting Polish classics and international favorites. **U Kucharzy**, a charming bistro in the Old Town, is a local favorite for its hearty pierogi and traditional Polish soups. **Butchery & Wine**, a trendy eatery in the Praga district, offers a unique dining concept that combines a butcher shop with a wine bar and restaurant.

Warsaw's diverse population has also brought a wealth of international flavors to the city. Savor the exotic spices of Indian cuisine at **Namaste India**, or indulge in the delicate flavors of Vietnamese pho at **Pho 206**. For a taste of Italy, head to **La Cantina**, a charming trattoria that serves up authentic pasta dishes and wood-fired pizzas.

No culinary exploration of Warsaw would be complete without a visit to a traditional milk bar (bar mleczny). These unpretentious establishments, with their simple decor and affordable prices, offer a taste of authentic

Polish home cooking. Try the pierogi ruskie at **Bar Mleczny Prasowy** in the Praga district, or savor the hearty bigos at **Bar Mleczny Bambino** in the city center.

## Market Delights: Hala Mirowska and Other Culinary Hubs

A symphony of sights, sounds, and aromas awaits at Warsaw's bustling markets, where the city's culinary soul comes alive. Step into Hala Mirowska, a vibrant indoor market housed in a historic Art Nouveau building, and prepare to be swept away by a sensory feast.

The air is thick with the mingled scents of fresh bread, ripe fruit, and exotic spices. Colorful stalls overflow with a cornucopia of local produce, from plump berries and sun-ripened tomatoes to artisanal cheeses and cured meats. The rhythmic chopping of knives, the lively chatter of vendors, and the cheerful bartering of shoppers create a symphony of sounds that hums with energy.

Wander through the maze of stalls and discover a treasure trove of culinary delights. Sample traditional Polish pierogi, their delicate dough encasing a variety of savory and sweet fillings. Indulge in freshly baked pastries, their golden crusts glistening with sugar. Savor the rich flavors of smoked fish, the tangy notes of pickled vegetables, and the vibrant hues of exotic spices.

Hala Mirowska is not just a market; it's a cultural microcosm, a place where locals and tourists alike gather to celebrate the simple pleasures of food and community. Pull up a stool at a bustling bar and sip on a frothy cappuccino or a shot of Polish vodka. Engage in conversation with the friendly vendors, eager to share their passion for their products.

Beyond Hala Mirowska, Warsaw boasts a variety of other culinary hubs worth exploring. The Hala Gwardii, a renovated market hall, offers a mix of traditional and modern vendors, while the Bazar Różyckiego, a sprawling outdoor market, is a treasure trove of antiques, collectibles, and vintage clothing.
No matter which market you choose to explore, prepare to be captivated by the vibrant atmosphere, tantalizing aromas, and diverse flavors that make Warsaw's culinary scene so unique.

# CHAPTER 4

## WARSAW'S CULTURAL SCENE

Warsaw's cultural scene is a vibrant and diverse mix of artistic expressions, where classical masterpieces and avant-garde creations coexist, inviting exploration and inspiration. From the elegant concert halls echoing with Chopin's melodies to the cutting-edge galleries showcasing Poland's most innovative artists, Warsaw's cultural scene is a testament to its enduring passion for the arts.

Immerse yourself in the city's theatrical traditions, where captivating performances unfold on stages steeped in history. Explore the world of Polish cinema, renowned for its poignant storytelling and artistic vision. Delve into the vibrant world of street art, where colorful murals and thought-provoking installations transform urban spaces into open-air galleries.

## Chopin's Legacy: Music in Warsaw

In Warsaw, the spirit of Frédéric Chopin dances on every breeze, his melodies echoing through the city's streets and concert halls. A native son and musical prodigy, Chopin's legacy is deeply intertwined with Warsaw's cultural identity, enriching its artistic tapestry with timeless compositions that continue to inspire and captivate.

Embark on a melodic journey through the city's musical landmarks, each a tribute to the maestro's genius. The Fryderyk Chopin Museum, housed in the elegant Ostrogski Palace, invites you to delve into the composer's life and works through a collection of personal artifacts, manuscripts, and musical instruments. Stroll through the museum's galleries, where interactive exhibits and multimedia displays bring Chopin's story to life.

In the heart of Łazienki Park, a bronze statue of Chopin graces the landscape, capturing the composer in a moment of quiet contemplation. As you wander through the park's idyllic gardens, imagine the young Chopin seeking inspiration amidst the tranquil surroundings, his melodies taking flight on the gentle breeze.

For a truly immersive experience, attend a Chopin concert at one of the city's many prestigious venues. The National Philharmonic Hall, with its exquisite acoustics and elegant ambiance, regularly hosts performances of Chopin's timeless compositions. During the summer months, the open-air theater in

Łazienki Park provides a magical setting for Chopin concerts under the stars.

Every five years, Warsaw comes alive with the prestigious International Chopin Piano Competition, a global showcase of musical talent that attracts aspiring pianists from around the world. Witness the passion and virtuosity of these young musicians as they interpret Chopin's masterpieces, breathing new life into his timeless melodies.

Beyond Chopin, Warsaw's musical landscape is a vibrant tapestry of genres and styles. Explore the city's diverse concert halls, jazz clubs, and music festivals, where you can discover emerging talents and experience the cutting-edge of Polish music. From classical to contemporary, Warsaw's musical scene offers something to delight every ear.

# The National Museum: Art and Artifacts of Poland

A grand repository of Poland's artistic and historical legacy, the National Museum in Warsaw stands as a cultural beacon, illuminating the nation's rich and diverse heritage. Within its stately halls, a vast collection of treasures awaits, spanning centuries of creativity and human ingenuity. From exquisite medieval artifacts to masterpieces of Renaissance painting, from evocative modern sculptures to thought-provoking contemporary installations, the museum offers a captivating journey through Poland's artistic and historical evolution.

Begin your exploration in the galleries dedicated to ancient art, where relics from the distant past offer glimpses into the lives and beliefs of Poland's early inhabitants. Marvel at intricately crafted jewelry, ornate weaponry, and ceremonial objects that whisper tales of ancient rituals and traditions.

As you move through the museum, you'll encounter a stunning array of Renaissance paintings, showcasing the artistic brilliance of Poland's Golden Age. Admire the works of renowned masters like Jan Matejko, whose monumental canvases depict historical events and national heroes with dramatic flair. Discover the delicate brushstrokes and vibrant colors of Stanisław Wyspiański's symbolist masterpieces, which capture the essence of Polish folklore and mythology.

The museum's modern and contemporary art collections offer a glimpse into Poland's artistic landscape of the 20th and 21st centuries. Explore the works of avant-garde artists who pushed boundaries and challenged conventions, as well as the creations of contemporary artists who continue to shape Poland's cultural identity.

**TO MAKE THE MOST OF YOUR VISIT, CONSIDER THE FOLLOWING TIPS:**

- **Allocate ample time:** The museum's vast collection requires a significant amount of time to fully appreciate. Plan to spend at least a few hours, or consider multiple visits if you have a particular interest in a specific period or genre.
- **Start with a guided tour:** Guided tours offer valuable insights into the museum's collections and themes, enriching your understanding of Polish art and history.
- **Focus on your interests:** With so much to see, it's helpful to prioritize the galleries that align with your personal interests. Consult the museum's map and floor plan to plan your route efficiently.
- **Take breaks:** The museum offers several cafes and restaurants where you can rest and refuel.
- **Ask questions:** The museum staff is knowledgeable and eager to share their expertise. Please do not hesitate to ask questions or seek recommendations.

**VISITOR INFORMATION:**

- **Address:** Al. Jerozolimskie 3, 00-495 Warszawa
- **Contact:** +48 22 621 10 31

- **Admission**: Tickets may be purchased online or at the museum's ticket office.
- **Guided Tours:** Available in various languages.
- **Accessibility:** The museum is totally accessible to people with impairments.

## Contemporary Art: Galleries and Street Art

A creative pulse surges through Warsaw, where contemporary art flourishes in galleries and spills onto the streets, transforming the urban landscape into a vibrant canvas. From thought-provoking installations to colorful murals that enliven building facades, the city's contemporary art scene is a testament to its innovative spirit and artistic expression.

Step into the Zachęta National Gallery of Art, a venerable institution that has championed Polish contemporary art for over a century. Here, you'll encounter a diverse collection of works by renowned Polish artists, as well as international figures who have left their mark on the global art scene. The gallery's ever-changing exhibitions showcase a wide range of artistic styles and mediums, from painting and sculpture to photography and multimedia installations. For a more experimental and avant-garde experience, venture to the Ujazdowski Castle Centre for

Contemporary Art. Housed in a historic castle complex, this dynamic institution is a hub of creative energy, hosting exhibitions, workshops, and discussions that push the boundaries of artistic expression. Explore thought-provoking installations that challenge traditional notions of art, and engage with artists and curators who are shaping the future of contemporary art in Poland.

Beyond the gallery walls, Warsaw's streets are a living testament to the city's artistic vibrancy. The Praga district, in particular, has become a hotbed of street art, with colorful murals and graffiti adorning its industrial buildings and hidden corners. Embark on a street art walking tour to discover these hidden gems, or simply wander through the neighborhood and let yourself be surprised by the unexpected artistic encounters that await.

Notable street art pieces to seek out include the "Kamień i co?" mural by Sainer and Bezt, a massive artwork that depicts a mysterious figure emerging from a rock face. The "Mr. Aryz" mural, located on the side of a residential building, is a whimsical depiction of a man balancing on a tightrope. And the "Rainbow Mural" by Natalia Rak, a vibrant celebration of diversity and acceptance, is a testament to the city's progressive spirit.

Warsaw's contemporary art scene is a dynamic and ever-evolving landscape, where creativity knows no bounds. From established galleries to impromptu street art exhibitions, the city offers a wealth of opportunities to engage with cutting-edge art and experience the pulse of Poland's creative spirit.

## Warsaw's Nightlife: Clubs, Bars, and Live Music Venues

As the sun dips below the horizon, Warsaw's vibrant energy ignites, transforming the city into a playground for night owls and revelers. Whether your ideal night out involves dancing to pulsating beats, sipping craft cocktails in a trendy bar, or enjoying live music in an intimate setting, Warsaw's diverse nightlife scene has something to satisfy every craving.

For those seeking a high-energy atmosphere, the clubs of Warsaw beckon with their pulsating beats and electrifying crowds. **Level 27**, perched atop a skyscraper, offers panoramic city views and a mix of house, techno, and hip-hop music. **Bank Club**, a veteran of the Warsaw nightlife scene, boasts one of the largest dance floors in the city and attracts top international DJs. **Newonce Bar**, located in the trendy Powiśle district, is a haven for electronic music lovers, with regular DJ sets and live performances.

If you prefer a more laid-back vibe, Warsaw's bars offer a diverse range of experiences. The **Old Town** is a popular spot for bar-hopping, with its charming cobblestone streets lined with pubs, cocktail bars, and traditional Polish vodka bars. **Pawilony**, a cluster of repurposed shipping containers, is a trendy spot for craft beer enthusiasts, with its numerous microbreweries and beer gardens.

For a taste of live music, head to the **Praga district**, where you'll find a variety of venues hosting everything from jazz and blues to rock and indie. **Hydrozagadka**, a former water pumping station, has been transformed into a unique cultural center that hosts concerts, exhibitions, and other events. **Klub SPATiF**, a legendary Warsaw institution, has been showcasing alternative music and culture since the 1980s.

Wherever your nocturnal adventures take you, remember to prioritize safety and etiquette. Warsaw is generally a safe city, but it's always wise to be aware of your surroundings and avoid walking alone in unfamiliar areas at night. Respect the local culture and customs, and be mindful of noise levels in residential areas. Most importantly, have fun and embrace the vibrant energy of Warsaw's nightlife!

# CHAPTER 5

## PRACTICALITIES & ESSENTIALS

Planning a trip to a new destination can be both exciting and daunting. To ensure your Warsaw adventure is nothing short of extraordinary, we've compiled essential information to help you navigate the city's practicalities with ease. From choosing the ideal time to visit and finding the perfect accommodation to mastering the intricacies of local currency and transportation, this chapter will equip you with the knowledge and resources necessary for a seamless and enjoyable travel experience.

Whether you're a seasoned globetrotter or a first-time visitor, our aim is to empower you with the tools to make informed decisions and create lasting memories in the vibrant Polish capital. So, let's dive into the practical aspects of your Warsaw journey, ensuring you're well-prepared to embrace all that this captivating city has to offer.

## Planning Your Visit: When to Go and How Long to Stay

Warsaw, with its continental climate, experiences distinct seasons, each offering a unique charm and appeal. When organizing your vacation, keep the following elements in mind to get the most out of it:

**BEST TIMES TO VISIT:**
- **Spring (April-May):** As the city awakens from its winter slumber, spring brings pleasant temperatures, blooming flowers, and a vibrant atmosphere. This is an ideal time for leisurely strolls through parks and gardens, outdoor cafes, and exploring the city's many cultural attractions.

- **Summer (June-August):** Warsaw's summers are warm and sunny, with average temperatures ranging from 20°C to 25°C (68°F to 77°F). This is peak tourist season, with numerous festivals and events taking place throughout the city. Prepare for more crowds and higher pricing during this period.

- **Autumn (September-October):** As the leaves turn golden, Warsaw takes on a magical aura. The weather is still pleasant, with mild temperatures and fewer crowds than in summer. This is a great time to explore the city's parks, enjoy outdoor activities, and savor the flavors of the harvest season.

- **Winter (November-March):** Warsaw's winters can be cold and snowy, with temperatures often dropping below freezing. However, the city transforms into a winter wonderland during this time, with festive markets, ice skating rinks, and twinkling lights.

## HOW LONG TO STAY

The ideal length of your stay in Warsaw depends on your interests and pace of travel. Here's a general guideline:

- **2-3 DAYS:** Perfect for a quick city break, allowing you to see the main highlights, such as the Old Town, the Royal Castle, and Łazienki Park. You'll also have time to sample some of the city's culinary delights and experience its nightlife.
- **4-5 DAYS:** Ideal for a more immersive experience, allowing you to explore beyond the city center and discover hidden gems. You can delve deeper into Warsaw's history and culture, visit some of its lesser-known museums and neighborhoods, and take a day trip to a nearby attraction.
- **1 WEEK OR MORE:** Perfect for those who want to fully immerse themselves in Warsaw's vibrant atmosphere and explore its surroundings. You can take your time discovering the city's many

facets, from its historical landmarks and cultural scene to its culinary delights and natural beauty. You can also embark on day trips to nearby towns and villages, such as Krakow, Gdansk, or the Wieliczka Salt Mine.

No matter how long you choose to stay, Warsaw is sure to leave a lasting impression with its rich history, vibrant culture, and warm hospitality.

## Accommodations: Hotels, Hostels, and Apartments

Warsaw offers a wide array of accommodations to suit every budget and travel style, ensuring a comfortable and enjoyable stay for all visitors. Whether you're seeking luxurious indulgence, budget-friendly options, or the comforts of home in a serviced apartment, the city's diverse lodging landscape has you covered.

**LUXURY HOTELS**

For those seeking refined elegance and impeccable service,

1. **H15 Boutique Hotel, Warsaw**
   - **Location:** Poznańska 15, 00-680 Warsaw, Poland
   - **Contact:** +48 22 55 387 00
   - **Email:** info@h15boutique.com

- **Description:** A 5-star hotel part of the Design Hotels collection, located in a historic building in the heart of Warsaw. It offers luxurious rooms and exceptional service.
- **Unique Features:** Historic significance, high-end amenities, and exceptional service.

2. **Radisson Collection Hotel, Warsaw**
    - **Location:** Grzybowska 24, 00-132 Warsaw, Poland
    - **Contact:** +48 22 321 88 88
    - **Email:** reservations.warsaw@radisson.com
    - **Description:** A high-standard hotel with a swimming pool, just a 10-minute walk from Warsaw Central Station. Offers air-conditioned rooms with tea and coffee facilities.
    - **Unique Features:** Proximity to central transport, luxurious facilities, and spacious rooms.

3. **InterContinental Warszawa, an IHG Hotel**
    - **Location:** Emilii Plater 49, 00-125 Warsaw, Poland
    - **Contact:** +48 22 328 88 88

- **Email:** icwarsaw@ihg.com
- **Description:** A 5-star hotel centrally located just 500 meters from Warsaw Central Station. Features include a swimming pool, fitness center, and sauna.
- **Unique Features:** Central location, luxury amenities, and excellent breakfast.

**MID-RANGE HOTELS**

Warsaw's mid-range hotels offer a comfortable and convenient stay without breaking the bank.

1. **Hotel Indigo Warsaw Nowy Świat, an IHG Hotel**
    - **Location:** Smolna 40, 00-375 Warsaw, Poland
    - **Contact:** +48 22 418 89 00
    - **Email:** indigo@ihg.com
    - **Description:** A boutique 4-star hotel in a renovated 19th-century building, opposite the National Museum. Known for its welcoming staff and fabulous rooms.
    - **Unique Features:** Historical building, central location, and boutique charm.

2. **Moxy Warsaw Praga**
    - **Location:** Ząbkowska 29, 03-736 Warsaw, Poland
    - **Contact:** +48 22 104 24 00
    - **Email:** info@moxywarsawpraga.com
    - **Description:** Located in the vibrant Praga district, this hotel offers modern accommodations and is a 10-minute walk from the Warszawa Wileńska subway station.
    - **Unique Features:** Modern design, vibrant neighborhood, and budget-friendly luxury.

**BUDGET HOTELS AND HOSTELS**

For budget-conscious travelers, Warsaw's hostels provide a social and affordable alternative.

1. **Planet Hostel**
    - **Location:** Marszałkowska 1, 00-624 Warsaw, Poland
    - **Contact:** +48 22 621 19 92
    - **Email:** planet@hostel.com
    - **Description:** Located near the city center, this hostel offers clean, budget-friendly rooms with shared kitchen facilities and free Wi-Fi.

- **Unique Features:** Central location, affordable pricing, and friendly atmosphere.

2. **Hostel Maxim**
    - **Location:** Targowa 41, 03-728 Warsaw, Poland
    - **Contact:** +48 22 670 37 91
    - **Email:** maxim@hostel.com
    - **Description:** Situated in the Praga-Północ district, near Warsaw East Train Station. Offers budget accommodations with shared facilities.
    - **Unique Features:** Proximity to public transport, clean environment, and helpful staff.

## APARTMENTS

If you prefer the comforts of home, consider staying in a serviced apartment.

1. **Warsaw Premium Apartments Old Town**
    - **Location:** Various locations in Old Town, Warsaw, Poland
    - **Contact:** +48 606 313 451
    - **Email:** premium@apartments.pl
    - **Description:** Offers premium apartments with kitchen facilities, close to

major attractions like the Barbican and Grand Theatre.
- **Unique Features:** Spacious apartments, prime locations, and high guest ratings.

2. **Platinum Apartments**
    - **Location:** Grzybowska 61, 00-855 Warsaw, Poland
    - **Contact:** +48 22 100 31 40
    - **Email:** info@platinumapartments.pl
    - **Description:** These apartments provide modern accommodations with free Wi-Fi and private parking, close to the Warsaw Uprising Monument.
    - **Unique Features:** Modern amenities, private entrances, and convenient locations.

Whether you're looking for luxury, mid-range, or budget accommodations, Warsaw offers a variety of options to suit every traveler's needs and preferences.

# Money Matters: Currency, Banking, and Tipping

In Poland, the official currency is the Polish Złoty (PLN), denoted by the symbol "zł." Familiarizing yourself with the currency and its denominations is essential for a smooth and hassle-free experience during your travels.

**EXCHANGE RATES AND CURRENCY EXCHANGE**
The exchange rate between the Polish Złoty and your home currency will fluctuate, so it's advisable to check the current rates before your trip. You can exchange your currency for Złoty at various locations, including:
- **Currency exchange bureaus (kantors):** These are widely available throughout Warsaw, offering competitive rates and convenient service.
- **Banks:** Banks also offer currency exchange services, but their rates may be less favorable than those at exchange bureaus.
- **ATMs:** Withdrawing Złoty directly from ATMs is often the most convenient and cost-effective option. However, be mindful of any costs your bank may impose for foreign transactions.

**USING ATMS AND CREDIT CARDS**
ATMs are ubiquitous in Warsaw, and most accept major international cards. Look for ATMs located in secure locations, such as banks or shopping centers. Inform your bank of your trip intentions to prevent having your card stopped.

Credit cards are generally accepted at hotels, restaurants, and bigger retail outlets. However, smaller establishments and markets may prefer cash, so it's always a good idea to carry some Złoty with you.

**TIPPING CUSTOMS**

Tipping is not mandatory in Poland, but it is customary to round up the bill in restaurants and cafes, or to leave a small amount of change. If you're particularly pleased with the service, a tip of 10-15% is appreciated.

In taxis, it's customary to round up the fare to the nearest Złoty or leave a small tip. For other services, such as hotel porters or hairdressers, a small tip is also appreciated.

By understanding the nuances of Polish currency and tipping customs, you can navigate your financial transactions with confidence and ensure a smooth and enjoyable travel experience.

# Getting There and Away: Flights, Trains, and Buses

Warsaw, the capital of Poland, is a major transportation hub in Central Europe, offering a variety of options for travelers arriving from different parts of the world. Here's an overview of the main transportation options for reaching Warsaw:

## BY AIR
### Chopin Airport (WAW)
- **Location:** 10 km south-west of the city center
- **Description:** The primary international airport serving Warsaw, handling the majority of the city's air traffic.
- **Airlines:** LOT Polish Airlines (flag carrier), Lufthansa, British Airways, Air France, and many low-cost carriers like Ryanair and Wizz Air.
- **Facilities:** Multiple terminals with a range of amenities including lounges, restaurants, shops, and transportation links to the city.

### Modlin Airport (WMI)
- **Location:** 40 km north-west of Warsaw
- **Description:** Mainly serves low-cost carriers and charter flights.
- **Airlines:** Ryanair and other budget airlines.
- **Facilities:** Smaller than Chopin Airport but provides essential services including car rentals and shuttle buses to Warsaw.

## BY TRAIN
### Warsaw Central Station (Warszawa Centralna)
- **Location:** Aleje Jerozolimskie 54, 00-024 Warsaw, Poland

- **Description:** The main railway station in Warsaw, well-connected with national and international routes.
- **Train Operators:** PKP Intercity (domestic and international services), EuroCity, and regional operators.
- **Routes:** Direct connections to major European cities like Berlin, Vienna, and Prague. Domestic routes include Kraków, Gdańsk, and Wrocław.
- **Facilities:** Shops, restaurants, waiting rooms, and easy access to public transportation.

**Warsaw West Station (Warszawa Zachodnia)**
- **Location:** Al. Jerozolimskie 144, 02-305 Warsaw, Poland
- **Description:** Another major train station catering to domestic and some international routes.
- **Train Operators:** Similar services to those at Warsaw Central Station.
- **Facilities:** Basic amenities including waiting areas and food outlets.

**BY BUS**

**Warsaw Bus Terminal (Dworzec Autobusowy Warszawa Zachodnia)**
- **Location:** Al. Jerozolimskie 144, 02-305 Warsaw, Poland

- **Description:** The main bus terminal in Warsaw, adjacent to Warsaw West Train Station.
- **Bus Operators:** FlixBus, PolskiBus, Lux Express, and other regional and international bus services.
- **Routes:** Extensive network covering domestic routes as well as international destinations such as Berlin, Vilnius, and Budapest.
- **Facilities:** Ticket offices, waiting areas, food vendors, and connections to other forms of public transport.

## AIRLINES SERVING WARSAW

- **LOT Polish Airlines:** The national carrier, offering numerous direct flights to European, North American, and Asian destinations.
- **Ryanair:** A prominent low-cost airline with connections primarily to European cities.
- **Lufthansa, British Airways, Air France:** Major international carriers with frequent flights to and from Warsaw.

## TRAIN SERVICES

- **PKP Intercity:** Provides high-speed and regular services across Poland and to neighboring countries.
- **EuroCity:** International train services connecting Warsaw with major European cities.

- **Regional Trains:** Serve local routes within Poland, offering an affordable and scenic travel option.

**BUS COMPANIES**
- **FlixBus:** Offers extensive domestic and international routes at competitive prices.
- **PolskiBus:** Known for its affordable services across Poland and to neighboring countries.
- **Lux Express:** Provides comfortable international bus travel with modern amenities.

Whether you're arriving by air, train, or bus, Warsaw offers a comprehensive range of transportation options to ensure a smooth journey to and from the city.

# Getting Around: Public Transportation and Taxis

Warsaw boasts an efficient and extensive public transportation network that seamlessly connects the city's diverse neighborhoods and attractions. Buses, trams, metro lines, and suburban trains offer convenient and affordable options for navigating the city, making it easy to explore Warsaw.

**PUBLIC TRANSPORTATION**

The metro, with its two lines (M1 and M2), is the fastest and most efficient way to traverse the city. Trains run frequently, and the system is well-maintained and easy to navigate. Trams offer a more scenic journey, winding through the streets and providing glimpses of Warsaw's architectural gems. Buses, with their extensive network, reach even the most remote corners of the city, ensuring accessibility for all.

**TICKETING**
Purchasing tickets for public transport is straightforward. Ticket machines are available at most stops and stations, accepting both cash and card payments. You can also purchase tickets through mobile apps like Jakdojade or mPay, which offer a convenient and contactless option.

Tickets are based on time validity, with options ranging from 20-minute to 90-minute passes, as well as day passes and multi-day passes for frequent travelers. Validate your ticket upon boarding the vehicle or entering the metro station to avoid fines.

**ROUTES AND NAVIGATION:**
Warsaw's public transportation routes are well-mapped and easy to understand. You can find detailed route maps at stops and stations, or use online resources and mobile apps to plan your journey. The Jakdojade

app, for example, provides real-time information on departures, arrivals, and delays.

**TAXIS AND RIDE-HAILING APPS**
Taxis are readily available throughout Warsaw, and can be hailed on the street or booked through apps like Uber or Bolt. When using taxis, ensure the meter is activated or agree on a fare upfront to avoid any misunderstandings. Ride-hailing apps offer a convenient and often more affordable alternative, allowing you to track your ride and pay electronically.

**BIKE RENTALS**
For those seeking a more active and eco-friendly mode of transportation, Warsaw offers numerous bike rental options. The city's extensive network of bike paths and lanes makes cycling a safe and enjoyable way to explore. Veturilo, Warsaw's bike-sharing system, allows you to rent bikes from numerous stations throughout the city using a mobile app.

**TIPS FOR NAVIGATING PUBLIC TRANSPORT**
- **Plan your journey in advance:** Use online resources or mobile apps to map your route and check schedules.
- **Validate your ticket:** Remember to validate your ticket upon boarding or entering the station.

- **Be mindful of peak hours:** Public transport can get crowded during rush hour, so plan accordingly.
- **Ask for help:** If you're unsure of which route to take or how to purchase a ticket, don't hesitate to ask a local or a transportation staff member for assistance.

With its well-connected public transportation system, readily available taxis, and numerous bike rental options, getting around Warsaw is a breeze.

# CHAPTER 6

## WARSAW'S NEIGHBORHOODS

Beyond the well-trodden paths of Warsaw's city center lies a mosaic of unique neighborhoods, each with its own distinct personality and allure. From the artistic haven of Praga to the tranquil charm of Żoliborz, these diverse enclaves offer a glimpse into the city's vibrant tapestry and invite you to discover hidden gems and local secrets.

Venture beyond the familiar and immerse yourself in the rich tapestry of Warsaw's neighborhoods, where the city's true character and spirit come alive. Whether you're seeking bohemian vibes, historical charm, or family-friendly fun, these diverse enclaves offer a wealth of experiences waiting to be discovered.

## Praga District: Warsaw's Edgy and Creative Side

On the eastern bank of the Vistula River, a vibrant energy pulses through the streets of Praga, a district that embodies Warsaw's edgy and creative spirit. Once a gritty industrial area, Praga has undergone a remarkable transformation, emerging as a haven for artists, musicians, and free thinkers. Its cobblestone streets, adorned with colorful murals and graffiti, exude an alternative vibe that's both gritty and inspiring.

Praga's industrial heritage is evident in its red-brick factories and warehouses, many of which have been repurposed into trendy studios, galleries, and performance spaces. The Soho Factory, a former vodka distillery, is now a bustling creative hub, hosting a variety of cultural events, exhibitions, and workshops. Its eclectic mix of shops, cafes, and restaurants makes it a popular destination for both locals and visitors.

Neon Muzeum, a glowing tribute to the communist era, is a must-visit for anyone interested in Warsaw's recent past. Housed in a former factory, the museum's collection of vintage neon signs illuminates the city's streets with a nostalgic glow. The signs, once ubiquitous during the communist era, now serve as a reminder of a bygone era and a testament to the city's evolving identity.

Koneser Praga Center, a revitalized vodka distillery complex, is another testament to Praga's creative spirit. The center houses a variety of cultural institutions, including the Polish Vodka Museum, the Google for Startups Campus, and numerous art galleries and design studios. Its vibrant mix of shops, restaurants, and event spaces makes it a popular destination for both locals and visitors.

As night falls, Praga's energy intensifies, with a thriving nightlife scene that caters to all tastes. From intimate jazz clubs to underground techno venues, the district's diverse offerings ensure a memorable night out. Whether you're sipping craft cocktails in a trendy bar or dancing the night away to live music, Praga's nightlife is sure to leave you wanting more.

Praga is a district that defies easy categorization. It's a place where the old and new collide, where industrial heritage meets artistic innovation, and where a gritty past gives way to a vibrant future.

## Żoliborz: A Leafy Residential Enclave

Escape the urban bustle and find solace in Żoliborz, a tranquil residential enclave nestled amidst lush greenery and charming architecture. This peaceful neighborhood, located just north of the city center, offers a respite from the hustle and bustle, inviting leisurely strolls along tree-lined streets and moments of quiet reflection in its many parks and gardens.

Żoliborz is renowned for its historic villas, many of which date back to the early 20th century. These elegant homes, with their intricate facades and manicured gardens, exude a timeless charm and offer a glimpse into the neighborhood's affluent past. As you wander through the quiet streets, you'll encounter a variety of architectural styles, from Art Deco to modernist, each contributing to the neighborhood's unique character.

Families will appreciate Żoliborz's welcoming atmosphere and abundance of green spaces. The Warsaw Citadel, a 19th-century fortress, now houses a museum dedicated to the city's history. The Żoliborz Artists' House, a cultural center housed in a former villa, hosts exhibitions, workshops, and other events throughout the year. And Kępa Potocka, a picturesque park on the banks of the Vistula River, offers a tranquil escape for nature lovers.

For a taste of local life, head to the Plac Wilsona, a bustling square lined with shops, cafes, and restaurants. Here, you can mingle with locals, enjoy a leisurely meal, or simply watch the world go by.

Żoliborz is a neighborhood that invites you to slow down, breathe deeply, and appreciate the simple pleasures of life. Whether you're strolling through its leafy streets, exploring its historic villas, or enjoying a picnic in one of its parks, Żoliborz is sure to charm you with its tranquil atmosphere and timeless beauty.

**VISITOR INFORMATION:**
- **Address:** Żoliborz district, Warsaw
- **Contact:** N/A (Residential neighborhood)
- **Hours:** Open 24 hours
- **Admission:** Free
- **Guided Tours:** Not typically available, but you can explore the neighborhood on your own or with a private guide.

**TIPS FOR VISITORS**
- **Take a leisurely stroll:** Explore the neighborhood's charming streets and admire its architecture.
- **Visit the Warsaw Citadel:** Learn about the city's history at this former fortress turned museum.
- **Explore the Żoliborz Artists' House:** Discover local art and culture at this vibrant cultural center.
- **Relax in Kępa Potocka:** Enjoy a picnic, go for a walk, or simply soak up the sun in this picturesque park.
- **Dine at Plac Wilsona:** Sample local cuisine and mingle with locals at this bustling square.

# Mokotów: Parks, Cafes, and Family-Friendly Vibes

Mokotów, a vibrant district pulsating with modern energy, invites you to experience Warsaw's contemporary side. Known for its sprawling parks, trendy cafes, and upscale shopping destinations, this dynamic enclave offers a vibrant mix of leisure, entertainment, and urban sophistication.

A haven for outdoor enthusiasts, Mokotów boasts an abundance of green spaces that offer a refreshing escape from the city's hustle and bustle. Pole Mokotowskie Park, the district's largest park, is a popular destination for joggers, cyclists, and families. Its sprawling lawns, tranquil ponds, and shaded pathways provide a serene setting for picnics, leisurely strolls, and outdoor activities.

For a taste of Warsaw's café culture, Mokotów offers a plethora of trendy establishments where you can savor a steaming cup of coffee or indulge in a delicious pastry. Wander along the district's charming streets and discover hidden gems like **Ministerstwo Kawy**, a coffee lover's paradise, or **Charlotte Menora**, a cozy French-inspired bistro.

Shopaholics will find their haven at Galeria Mokotów, one of the city's largest shopping centers. With its vast array of international brands, designer boutiques, and trendy restaurants, this upscale destination caters to every taste and budget.

Mokotów's appeal extends to families and young professionals alike. Its well-maintained parks and playgrounds provide ample space for children to play, while its proximity to business centers and universities makes it a convenient and desirable place to live. The district's lively atmosphere, diverse cultural scene, and abundance of amenities create a vibrant and welcoming community for residents and visitors alike.

**VISITOR INFORMATION**
- **Address:** Mokotów district, Warsaw
- **Contact:** N/A (Residential and commercial district)
- **Hours:** Varies by establishment
- **Admission:** Free (except for specific attractions and events)

**TIPS FOR VISITORS**
- **Explore Pole Mokotowskie Park:** Enjoy a leisurely walk, bike ride, or picnic in this sprawling green oasis.

- **Discover Mokotów's cafe culture:** Sample the offerings at the district's many trendy cafes and bistros.
- **Indulge in retail therapy:** Shop till you drop at Galeria Mokotów, one of Warsaw's largest shopping centers.
- **Experience the district's nightlife:** Mokotów boasts a lively bar and restaurant scene, perfect for a night out.
- **Embrace the local vibe:** Mingle with residents and soak up the atmosphere of this dynamic district.

## Ochota: A Blend of Old and New

A harmonious blend of history and modernity, Ochota invites you to explore its diverse landscape where the echoes of the past intertwine with the pulse of the present. This dynamic district, nestled just west of the city center, offers a fascinating mix of architectural styles, cultural attractions, and recreational spaces, making it a captivating destination for both locals and visitors.

History buffs will find themselves drawn to the Warsaw Uprising Museum, a poignant tribute to the heroic resistance fighters of 1944. Through immersive exhibits, personal stories, and multimedia displays, the museum transports visitors back in time, recounting the bravery and sacrifice of those who fought for their city's freedom.

For those seeking retail therapy, Blue City, one of Warsaw's largest shopping centers, beckons with its vast array of shops, boutiques, and restaurants. From international fashion brands to local Polish designers, this modern shopping complex caters to every taste and budget.

After a day of exploring, unwind in Szczęśliwicki Park, a sprawling green oasis that offers a welcome respite from the urban bustle. Stroll along its tranquil paths, rent a paddleboat on the lake, or simply relax on a bench and soak up the sun. In winter, the park transforms into a winter wonderland, with a popular ski slope and ice skating rink drawing crowds of all ages.

Ochota's convenient location, just a short tram or bus ride from the city center, makes it an ideal base for exploring Warsaw. Its diverse mix of residential, commercial, and recreational areas ensures there's something for everyone in this dynamic district. Whether you're interested in history, shopping, or simply enjoying the outdoors, Ochota offers a unique and rewarding experience.

# CHAPTER 7

## OFF THE BEATEN PATH

Ditch the guidebook and embark on an adventure beyond the well-trodden tourist trails. Warsaw, a city of hidden depths and unexpected delights, invites you to uncover its lesser-known treasures, those tucked-away gems that reveal a different side of its character.

From quirky museums that celebrate the city's unique history and culture to offbeat neighborhoods brimming with local charm, Warsaw offers a wealth of experiences for those seeking a more authentic and unconventional journey. Leave the crowds behind and wander down cobblestone streets, discover hidden courtyards, and stumble upon quirky cafes and shops that will surprise and delight you.

Immerse yourself in the city's alternative scene, where artistic expression flourishes in unexpected places. Explore abandoned factories transformed into vibrant cultural centers, admire the colorful murals that adorn building facades, and discover the hidden stories behind the city's most intriguing landmarks.

This chapter is your passport to a Warsaw that few tourists get to see. So, put on your explorer's hat and prepare to be enchanted by the city's offbeat charm and hidden treasures.

## Neon Muzeum: A Glowing Tribute to Communist-Era Signage

Step into a time capsule of glowing nostalgia at the Neon Muzeum, a vibrant haven that pays homage to the artistry and historical significance of communist-era signage. Housed within a former factory in the Praga district, this unique museum showcases a dazzling collection of vintage neon signs that once illuminated Warsaw's streets, casting their colorful glow on a bygone era.

As you wander through the museum's labyrinthine halls, you'll be transported back in time to a period when neon signs were more than just advertisements; they were symbols of progress, optimism, and cultural identity. Each sign, with its distinct design and typography, tells a story of ingenuity, craftsmanship, and the artistic vision of a generation.

Admire the bold, geometric shapes of the "Kino Praha" sign, a beacon for moviegoers in the 1950s. Marvel at the intricate details of the "Supersam" sign, a testament to the era's fascination with consumerism. And let yourself be mesmerized by the mesmerizing glow of the "Berlin" sign, a reminder of Warsaw's cultural connections to the wider world.

The Neon Muzeum's mission goes beyond mere preservation; it seeks to illuminate the cultural context and historical significance of these iconic signs. Through exhibitions, educational programs, and interactive displays, the museum explores the role of neon signs in shaping Warsaw's urban landscape and reflecting the aspirations and anxieties of a society in flux.

Whether you're a design aficionado, a history buff, or simply curious about Warsaw's past, the Neon Muzeum offers a unique and illuminating experience. It's a place where the past comes alive in a blaze of neon, where the stories of a generation are told through the glowing letters and symbols that once defined a city.

**VISITOR INFORMATION**
- **Address:** Soho Factory, Mińska 25, 03-808 Warszawa
- **Contact:** +48 665 711 635
- **Hours:** Tuesday-Sunday, 11:00 AM - 5:00 PM
- **Admission:** Adults - 15 zł, Students/Seniors - 10 zł, Children under 7 - Free
- **Guided Tours:** Available in Polish and English.

**TIPS FOR VISITORS**
- **Take your time:** Allow ample time to explore the museum's diverse collection of neon signs.
- **Read the descriptions:** Each sign has a detailed description that provides historical context and insights into its design.
- **Take photos:** The museum encourages photography, so don't hesitate to capture your favorite signs.
- **Ask questions:** The museum staff is knowledgeable and passionate about neon signs, so feel free to ask questions.
- **Visit the gift shop:** Take home a piece of neon history with a souvenir from the museum's gift shop.

# The Warsaw Rising Museum: Stories of Resistance and Heroism

A solemn tribute to bravery and sacrifice, the Warsaw Rising Museum stands as a poignant reminder of a pivotal moment in the city's history. Step inside its hallowed halls and immerse yourself in the stories of courage, resilience, and unwavering hope that defined the Warsaw Uprising of 1944.

The museum's interactive exhibits transport you back in time, allowing you to walk through the streets of a war-torn city, hear the echoes of gunfire and explosions, and witness the indomitable spirit of the resistance fighters. Through personal accounts, photographs, and artifacts, the museum paints a vivid picture of the uprising, highlighting the sacrifices made by ordinary citizens who rose up against Nazi occupation.

Explore the underground bunkers where resistance fighters planned their strategies, witness the makeshift hospitals where the wounded were treated, and walk through the reconstructed streets where fierce battles raged. Hear the voices of survivors as they recount their harrowing experiences, their stories of resilience and hope resonating through the exhibits.

The Warsaw Rising Museum is more than just a collection of artifacts; it's a living testament to the human spirit's ability to overcome adversity. By preserving the memory of the uprising, the museum honors the sacrifices of those who fought for freedom and reminds us of the importance of standing up for what we believe in.

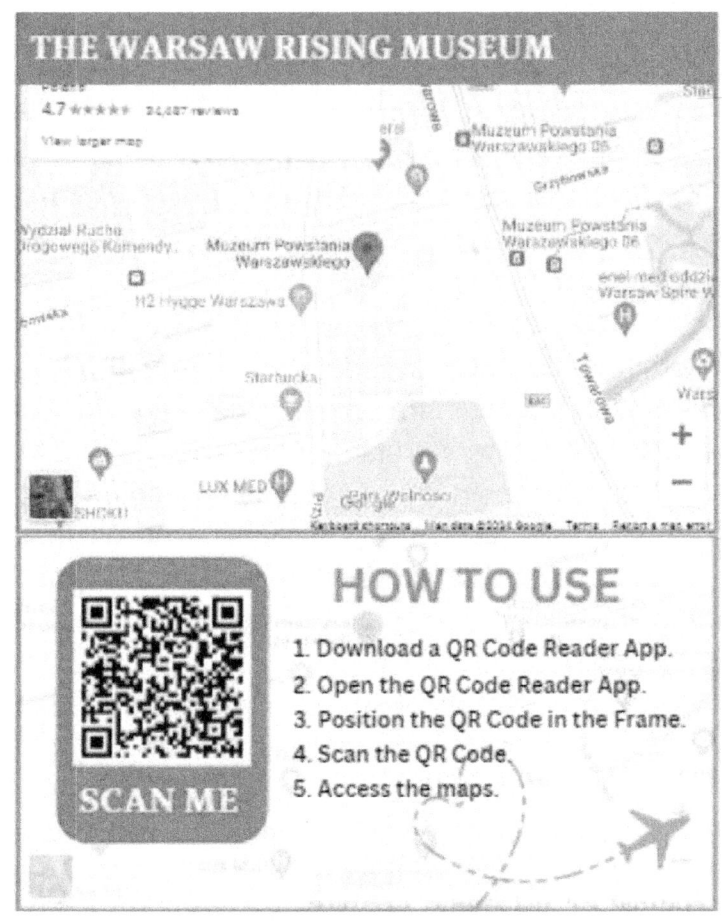

**VISITOR INFORMATION**
- **Address:** Grzybowska 79, 00-844 Warszawa
- **Contact:** +48 22 539 79 05

- **Hours:** vary according on the season and day of the week. Check the official website for the most up-to-date information.
- **Admission:** Tickets are available for purchase both online and in the museum's ticket office.
- **Guided Tours:** Available in various languages.
- **Accessibility:** The museum is fully accessible for visitors with disabilities.

**TIPS FOR VISITORS**
- **Allocate ample time:** Allow at least 2-3 hours to fully explore the museum's exhibits.
- **Start at the beginning:** The exhibition follows a chronological order, starting with the pre-war years and ending with the aftermath of the uprising.
- **Watch the films:** The museum features several short films that provide historical context and personal accounts of the uprising.
- **Listen to the audio recordings:** Many exhibits include audio recordings of survivors' testimonies, adding another layer of depth and emotion to the experience.
- **Reflect on the sacrifices:** The Warsaw Uprising was a pivotal moment in Polish history, and the museum offers a space for reflection and remembrance.

# Wilanów Palace: A Baroque Masterpiece on the Outskirts

A short journey from the heart of Warsaw reveals a vision of regal splendor: Wilanów Palace, a Baroque masterpiece that transports you to a bygone era of opulence and artistry. Nestled amidst sprawling gardens and tranquil lakes, this architectural gem beckons with its ornate facades, lavish interiors, and captivating history.

As you approach the palace, its imposing presence commands attention. The grand facade, adorned with statues, columns, and intricate details, reflects the splendor of the Baroque era. Step inside and be greeted by a world of gilded ceilings, ornate chandeliers, and opulent furnishings. Each room, a testament to the exquisite craftsmanship of the period, tells a story of royal life and cultural sophistication.

Wander through the palace's lavish apartments, where kings and queens once resided. Admire the King's Bedroom, with its ornate canopy bed and rich tapestries. Explore the Queen's Drawing Room, a haven of elegance and refinement. And marvel at the grandeur of the Great Hall, where lavish banquets and courtly ceremonies once took place.

The palace's gardens, a masterpiece of landscape design, are a feast for the senses. Stroll along manicured paths, admire the vibrant flower beds, and discover hidden grottoes and sculptures. The gardens, designed in the French style, offer a serene escape from the city's bustle, inviting you to linger and soak in the beauty of nature.

Wilanów Palace is not just a historical relic; it's a living testament to Poland's rich cultural heritage. The palace regularly hosts concerts, exhibitions, and other cultural events, ensuring that its legacy continues to thrive. Its collections of paintings, sculptures, and decorative arts offer a window into the artistic tastes and aspirations of the Polish nobility.

**VISITOR INFORMATION**
- **Address:** Stanisława Kostki Potockiego 10/16, 02-958 Warszawa
- **Contact:** +48 22 544 28 00
- **Hours:** vary according on the season and day of the week. Check the official website for the most up-to-date information.
- **Admission:** Tickets can be purchased online or at the palace's ticket office.
- **Guided Tours:** Available in various languages.
- **Accessibility:** The palace is partially accessible for visitors with disabilities.

**TIPS FOR VISITORS**
- **Visit the Palace Museum:** Explore the palace's rich collection of art and artifacts.
- **Stroll through the gardens:** Take your time to admire the beauty of the palace's meticulously manicured gardens.
- **Attend a cultural event:** Check the schedule for concerts, exhibitions, and other events taking place at the palace.
- **Enjoy a meal or a drink:** The palace has a café and restaurant where you can relax and refuel.
- **Take a guided tour:** Learn about the palace's history and architecture from a knowledgeable guide.

# The Vistula River: Recreation and Riverfront Views

The Vistula River, a shimmering ribbon that winds its way through the heart of Warsaw, offers a refreshing escape from the city's urban bustle. Its scenic riverfront areas, with their sandy beaches, lush parks, and inviting cafes, beckon both locals and visitors alike to unwind and embrace the slower pace of life.

Stroll along the revitalized boulevards that flank the river's edge, where cyclists, joggers, and rollerbladers glide past, their laughter mingling with the gentle lapping of waves. Find a secluded spot on the sandy beaches of Saska Kępa or Rusałka, where you can soak up the sun, build sandcastles with the kids, or simply relax with a good book.

For those seeking a more active adventure, rent a kayak or paddleboard and explore the river's tranquil waters. Join a guided boat cruise to admire the city's iconic landmarks from a different perspective, or simply rent a bike and pedal along the scenic bike paths that wind their way along the riverbank.

As the sun sets, the Vistula River transforms into a romantic haven, its waters shimmering with the city's reflected lights. Find a cozy spot at one of the many riverside cafes or restaurants and savor a delicious meal as you watch the sunset over the city's skyline.

**ACTIVITIES AND ATTRACTIONS**
- **Vistula Boulevards:** Stroll, cycle, or rollerblade along these revitalized boulevards, lined with cafes, bars, and restaurants.
- **Beaches:** Relax and soak up the sun on the sandy beaches of Saska Kępa or Rusałka.
- **Parks:** Enjoy the tranquility of the Skaryszewski Park or the Poniatówka Park, both located along the riverbank.

- **Boat cruises:** Take a leisurely cruise along the Vistula and admire Warsaw's landmarks from a different perspective.
- **Kayaking and paddleboarding:** Kayaking and paddleboarding: Rent a kayak or paddleboard and cruise the river at your leisure.
- **Riverside cafes and restaurants:** Savor a delicious meal or a refreshing drink while enjoying the river views.

# CHAPTER 8

## WARSAW FOR PHOTOGRAPHY ENTHUSIASTS

For the lens-wielding traveler, Warsaw unfolds as a canvas of captivating contrasts, a city where history and modernity intertwine to create a visual feast. From the majestic spires of the Royal Castle to the vibrant murals that adorn hidden alleyways, the city offers a wealth of photographic opportunities for both seasoned professionals and casual shutterbugs.

Capture the grandeur of Warsaw's architectural landmarks, their intricate details and imposing facades. Freeze the fleeting moments of everyday life in the bustling market squares and lively streets. Seek out the serene beauty of the city's parks and gardens, where nature's palette explodes in a riot of color and texture. Whether you're drawn to the city's historical sites, its modern architecture, its vibrant street life, or its tranquil natural settings, Warsaw offers endless inspiration for your photographic endeavors. So, grab your camera and embark on a visual journey through this captivating city, where every corner holds a potential masterpiece waiting to be captured.

# Rooftop Bars: Capture Warsaw's Skyline

Elevate your perspective and capture Warsaw's breathtaking skyline from the city's trendy rooftop bars, where panoramic views and stylish ambiance converge. These elevated oases offer a unique vantage point to capture the city's architectural wonders bathed in the golden hues of sunset or illuminated by the twinkling lights of the cityscape at night.

**Level 27:** Ascend to the highest bar in Poland and be mesmerized by the sweeping vistas that unfold before you. Located atop the Millennium Plaza skyscraper, Level 27 offers an unobstructed 360-degree view of Warsaw's cityscape. Sip on handcrafted cocktails as you capture the dynamic skyline, where historic landmarks mingle with modern skyscrapers. For optimal lighting, aim for the golden hour, when the warm sunlight casts a magical glow over the city.

**The View Sky Bar:** Nestled atop the Hotel Warszawa, this stylish rooftop bar offers a sophisticated ambiance and stunning views of the city's iconic landmarks, including the Palace of Culture and Science and the Old Town. Capture the dramatic contrast between the city's historic and modern architecture as you sip on a signature cocktail or savor a delectable dish from the bar's menu. Consider visiting at dusk, when the city lights twinkle against the darkening sky, creating a mesmerizing scene.

**Panorama Sky Bar:** Located on the 40th floor of the Marriott Hotel, this elegant bar offers a panoramic view of Warsaw's sprawling cityscape. Capture the city's diverse neighborhoods, from the historic Old Town to the modern business district, as you enjoy the bar's refined atmosphere and extensive drink menu. For a unique perspective, try capturing long-exposure shots of the city lights at night, creating a mesmerizing tapestry of color and movement.

## TIPS FOR CAPTURING THE PERFECT CITYSCAPE SHOT

**Golden Hour:** The hour after sunrise or before sunset offers the most flattering light for cityscape photography, casting a warm glow and creating long shadows.

**Blue Hour:** The hour after sunset, when the sky is a deep blue hue, can create dramatic and moody cityscape shots.

**Tripod:** Use a tripod to ensure sharp images, especially in low-light conditions.

**Wide-angle lens:** A wide-angle lens will allow you to capture more of the cityscape in a single frame.

**Composition:** Experiment with different angles and perspectives to create unique and visually interesting compositions.

With its diverse skyline and numerous rooftop bars, Warsaw offers endless opportunities for capturing stunning cityscape photos. So, grab your camera, head to one of these elevated havens, and let your creativity soar as you capture the city's beauty from above.

# Old Town Charm: Architectural Photography Tips

A photographer's paradise, Warsaw's Old Town is a treasure trove of architectural gems, each corner revealing a new perspective and captivating detail. From the colorful facades of merchant houses to the intricate brickwork of Gothic churches, this historic district offers a wealth of visual delights for those who know where to look.

As you wander through the Old Town's winding streets, be sure to capture the essence of its architectural character. Pay attention to the details: the ornate doorways, the weathered statues, the intricate ironwork balconies. Look for interesting patterns and textures in the brickwork, the cobblestones, and the rooftops.

The interaction of light and shadow may give depth and emotion to your photographs. Early morning and late afternoon light casts long shadows, highlighting the architectural details and creating a sense of mystery. Experiment with different angles and perspectives to capture unique and visually striking compositions.

Don't forget to capture the human element. The Old Town is a living, breathing community, and its residents are an integral part of its charm. Capture candid moments of people going about their daily lives, adding a touch of authenticity and vitality to your images.

## HERE ARE SOME SPECIFIC TIPS FOR CAPTURING THE OLD TOWN'S ARCHITECTURAL CHARM

- **Get up early:** The soft morning light is ideal for capturing the details of the architecture without harsh shadows.
- **Look for reflections:** The Old Town's many windows and puddles offer opportunities for capturing interesting reflections.
- **Use a wide-angle lens:** A wide-angle lens will allow you to capture more of the scene in a single frame.
- **Experiment with different angles:** Don't be afraid to get low to the ground or climb up high to capture unique perspectives.

- **Pay attention to the details:** The Old Town is full of small details that can make for interesting photos.

With its rich history and diverse architecture, the Old Town is a photographer's dream. So grab your camera, explore its charming streets, and let your creativity run wild as you capture the essence of this unique and captivating district.

## Street Scenes: Documenting Warsaw's Daily Life

Embrace the vibrant pulse of Warsaw's streets, where everyday moments unfold in a captivating ballet of human interaction. From the bustling energy of market squares to the quiet contemplation of a lone street musician, the city's street life offers a wealth of photographic opportunities for those seeking to capture the essence of Warsaw's soul.

Seek out the lively atmosphere of the **Old Town Market Square**, where locals and tourists mingle amidst the colorful facades and historic landmarks. Capture the joyful laughter of children playing, the animated conversations of friends catching up, and the quiet moments of contemplation on a park bench.

Venture into the **Praga district**, a haven for street art and bohemian vibes. Here, you'll find vibrant murals adorning building facades, street performers showcasing their talents, and a diverse mix of people going about their daily lives. Capture the raw energy and creative spirit of this up-and-coming neighborhood. Explore the bustling **Hala Mirowska market**, where the sights, sounds, and smells of fresh produce, local delicacies, and exotic spices create a sensory overload. Capture the vibrant colors of the market stalls, the animated interactions between vendors and shoppers, and the sheer joy of discovering new culinary treasures.

For a more intimate glimpse into Warsaw's street life, wander through the quiet residential neighborhoods. Observe the interactions between neighbors, the playful antics of children, and the everyday routines that make up the fabric of urban life.

**TIPS FOR CAPTURING THE ESSENCE OF STREET LIFE**
- **Blend in:** Dress casually and avoid drawing attention to yourself.
- **Be patient:** Take your time to observe the scene and wait for the right moment to capture the perfect shot.

- **Look for the unexpected:** The most interesting photos often capture the spontaneous and unscripted moments of daily life.
- **Focus on emotions:** Capture the joy, sorrow, surprise, or curiosity that play across people's faces.
- **Tell a story:** Use your photos to create a narrative that captures the essence of Warsaw's street life.

Warsaw's streets are a living, breathing canvas, waiting to be captured through your lens. So grab your camera, venture out into the urban jungle, and let the city's vibrant energy inspire your photographic creativity.

## Parks and Gardens: Nature Photography Opportunities

Escape the urban bustle and immerse yourself in Warsaw's verdant oases, where nature's artistry unfolds in a symphony of colors, textures, and fleeting moments. The city's parks and gardens offer a haven for nature photographers, their diverse landscapes providing endless opportunities to capture the beauty of the natural world.

Łazienki Park, a sprawling expanse of manicured lawns, tranquil lakes, and ornate palaces, is a photographer's paradise. Capture the vibrant hues of blooming flowers, the graceful silhouettes of swans gliding across the water, and the majestic presence of ancient trees. The park's diverse flora and fauna offer a wealth of subjects, from delicate butterflies flitting among the blossoms to playful squirrels scampering through the undergrowth.

Saxon Garden, a historic park located in the heart of the city, boasts geometrically patterned flower beds, sculpted hedges, and a picturesque fountain. Its formal design and meticulously maintained lawns create a sense of order and harmony, providing a striking contrast to the surrounding urban landscape.

The Royal Baths Park, a hidden gem nestled on the banks of the Vistula River, offers a wilder and more natural setting. Its winding paths lead through dense forests, where sunlight filters through the leaves, creating a dappled tapestry of light and shadow. Capture the vibrant colors of autumn foliage, the delicate beauty of spring wildflowers, or the stark elegance of winter landscapes.

## TIPS FOR PHOTOGRAPHING NATURE IN WARSAW

- **Golden Hour:** The hour after sunrise or before sunset offers the most flattering light for nature photography, casting a warm glow and creating long shadows.
- **Macro Lens:** Use a macro lens to capture the intricate details of flowers, insects, and other small subjects.
- **Wide-angle Lens:** A wide-angle lens is ideal for capturing sweeping landscapes and panoramic views.
- **Polarizing Filter:** A polarizing filter can help reduce glare and enhance the colors of foliage and water.
- **Patience:** Take your time to observe the environment and wait for the right moment to capture the perfect shot.

Warsaw's parks and gardens offer endless possibilities for nature photography. So grab your camera, explore these verdant oases, and let the beauty of the natural world inspire your creativity.

# CHAPTER 9

## STAYING SAFE & ETIQUETTE

Embarking on any adventure requires a sense of preparedness, and your journey through Warsaw is no exception. While the city is known for its welcoming atmosphere and friendly locals, being informed and culturally aware will enhance your experience and ensure a safe and enjoyable stay. This chapter equips you with essential tips for navigating Warsaw's streets, staying healthy, and respecting local customs. From health precautions and emergency contacts to cultural nuances and etiquette tips, consider this your guide to a worry-free and enriching exploration of the Polish capital.

By prioritizing your well-being and embracing cultural sensitivity, you'll not only ensure a smooth journey but also foster meaningful connections with the people and places you encounter. So, let's delve into the practicalities of staying safe and respecting the local way of life, paving the way for a truly enriching and memorable Warsaw experience.

# Health and Safety Tips for Travelers

Embarking on your Warsaw adventure should be filled with excitement and wonder, not worry. By taking a few simple precautions and being mindful of your health and safety, you can ensure a smooth and enjoyable journey.

**BEFORE YOU GO**
- **Vaccinations:** Ensure you are up-to-date on routine vaccinations, such as measles, mumps, rubella, and diphtheria. Consult your doctor or a travel clinic for advice on any additional vaccinations that may be recommended for Poland.
- **Travel Insurance:** A comprehensive travel insurance policy will provide peace of mind and cover you in case of unexpected medical expenses, trip cancellations, or lost luggage.

**DURING YOUR TRIP**
- **Food and Water Safety:** Tap water in Warsaw is safe to drink, but bottled water is readily available if you prefer. Be cautious of street food vendors and choose establishments with good hygiene practices. Wash your hands often, particularly before eating.

- **Petty Theft:** Like any major city, petty theft can be an issue in Warsaw. Be mindful of your belongings in crowded areas, keep your valuables secure, and avoid flashing large amounts of cash.
- **Emergency Services:** In case of an emergency, dial 112 for the integrated emergency service (police, fire, ambulance). For non-emergency medical assistance, visit a local pharmacy (apteka) or seek help at a hospital or clinic.

## HEALTH CONCERNS

- **Air Quality:** Warsaw's air quality can be poor at times, especially during the winter months. If you have respiratory issues, consider wearing a mask or limiting outdoor activities on days with high pollution levels.
- **Ticks:** If you plan on spending time in wooded areas, be aware of ticks, which can transmit diseases such as Lyme disease. Wear long sleeves and pants, use insect repellent, and check yourself for ticks after being outdoors.

By taking these simple precautions and being mindful of your health and safety, you can focus on enjoying all that Warsaw has to offer. Remember, a little preparation goes a long way in ensuring a smooth and worry-free travel experience.

## Cultural Norms and Etiquette in Warsaw

Navigating a new culture is a rewarding experience, but it's essential to be mindful of local customs and etiquette to ensure respectful interactions and avoid any unintended faux pas. In Warsaw, as in any city, understanding cultural norms is key to fostering positive connections and making the most of your visit.

**GREETINGS AND INTRODUCTIONS**
- When meeting someone for the first time, a handshake is the customary greeting. Maintain eye contact and offer a firm handshake while saying "dzień dobry" (good morning/day) or "dobry wieczór" (good evening).
- When addressing someone, use their title (Pan for Mr., Pani for Mrs./Ms.) followed by their last name. Only switch to first names if invited to do so.
- Poles generally value personal space, so avoid excessive physical contact or overly familiar gestures.

## DRESS CODE
- While Warsaw is a cosmopolitan city with diverse fashion styles, it's generally considered polite to dress modestly, especially when visiting churches or religious sites.
- Avoid overly casual attire, such as shorts and flip-flops, in more formal settings like restaurants and theaters.

## TABLE MANNERS
- When dining out, wait to be seated by the host or hostess.
- Keep your hands visible above the table while eating.
- Avoid talking with your mouth full and use utensils to eat, even for pizza or sandwiches.
- It is considered courteous to finish everything on your plate.
- If you're invited to a Polish home, bring a small gift for the host, such as flowers, chocolates, or a bottle of wine.

## GIFT-GIVING CUSTOMS:
- When giving flowers, an odd number is preferred, except for funerals where an even number is appropriate.
- Avoid giving chrysanthemums, as they are associated with funerals.

- If you're invited to a Polish home, a small gift for the host is always appreciated.

**INTERACTIONS WITH LOCALS**
- Poles are generally polite and reserved. Avoid being too loud or raucous in public.
- Learn a few basic Polish phrases. Even a simple "dziękuję" (thank you) will be appreciated.
- Show respect for the city's history and culture by avoiding sensitive topics, such as politics or religion.
- Be patient and understanding of cultural differences. Not everyone may speak English, so gestures and smiles can go a long way.

**COMMON FAUX PAS TO AVOID**
Don't wear shoes indoors in someone's home.
- Avoid making jokes about Polish history or culture.
- Don't point your finger at someone; it's considered rude.
- Don't refuse a drink or food offered by a host; it's considered impolite.

By following these tips and embracing the local culture, you can ensure a respectful and enjoyable experience in Warsaw. Remember, a little cultural sensitivity goes a long way in building bridges and creating lasting memories.

## Emergency Contacts and Information

In case of any emergency during your stay in Warsaw, it's crucial to have access to reliable information and contact numbers. Here's a comprehensive list to ensure your safety and well-being:

**EMERGENCY NUMBERS:**
- **112:** This is the general emergency number for Poland, connecting you to the police, fire department, and ambulance services.
- **999:** Ambulance
- **998:** Fire Department
- **997:** Police

**TOURIST ASSISTANCE:**
- **Warsaw Tourist Information Center:** +48 22 194 31
- **Tourist Police:** +48 22 603 74 55 (available 24/7)

**EMBASSIES AND CONSULATES:**
Most countries have embassies or consulates in Warsaw, providing assistance to their citizens in case of emergencies or lost documents. Check the website

of your embassy or consulate for contact information and opening hours.

**MEDICAL FACILITIES:**

Warsaw boasts a well-developed healthcare system with numerous hospitals and clinics. In case of a medical emergency, seek assistance at the nearest hospital or call for an ambulance.

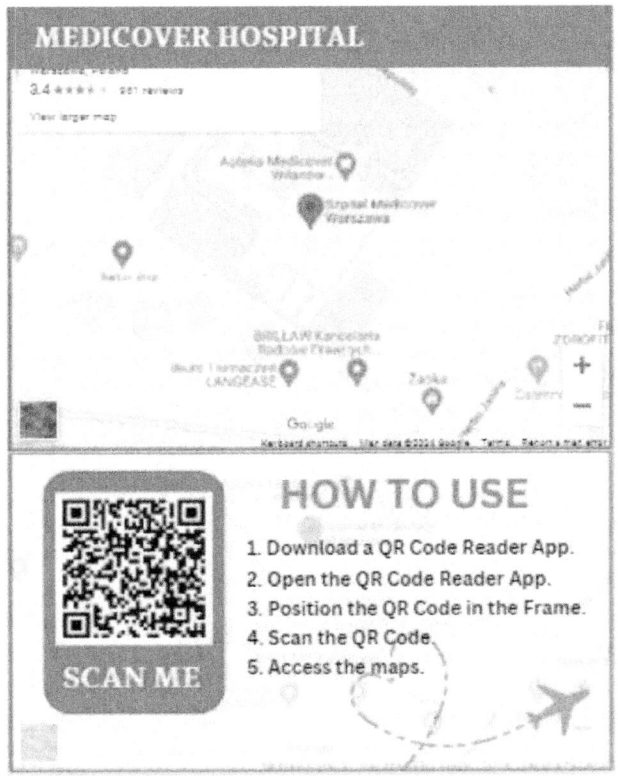

- **Medicover Hospital:** +48 22 439 20 00
- **Central Clinical Hospital of the Ministry of Interior and Administration:** +48 22 831 10 01
- **Independent Public Central Clinical Hospital:** +48 22 851 90 01

## RESOURCES FOR TRAVELERS WITH DISABILITIES:

- **Warsaw Tourist Information Center:** The center can provide information on accessible transportation, accommodation, and attractions.
- **Integration Foundation:** This organization offers assistance and resources for people with disabilities.

## ADDITIONAL TIPS:

- **Save important numbers:** Keep a list of emergency contacts and important phone numbers in your phone or wallet.
- **Learn basic Polish phrases:** Knowing a few basic phrases, such as "pomocy" (help) and "potrzebuję lekarza" (I need a doctor), can be helpful in an emergency.
- **Register with your embassy:** If you're staying in Warsaw for an extended period, consider registering with your embassy or consulate This

will make it easier for them to reach you in the event of an emergency.

By being prepared and informed, you can ensure a safe and enjoyable trip to Warsaw. Remember, it's always better to err on the side of caution and seek help if you need it.

# CHAPTER 10

**DAY TRIPS & EXCURSIONS**

While Warsaw's allure is undeniable, the surrounding region beckons with a treasure trove of diverse experiences. Escape the urban bustle and embark on a day trip to discover charming towns steeped in history, poignant memorials that honor a somber past, and breathtaking natural landscapes that rejuvenate the soul.

From the haunting beauty of Treblinka to the musical legacy of Żelazowa Wola, these excursions offer a deeper understanding of Poland's rich heritage and a chance to connect with its diverse landscapes and cultural traditions. Whether you're seeking historical immersion, natural beauty, or simply a change of pace, these day trips from Warsaw promise unforgettable experiences that will enrich your Polish adventure.

## Treblinka Memorial: A Solemn Reminder

A place of profound sorrow and remembrance, the Treblinka Memorial stands as a solemn testament to the horrors of the Holocaust. Located about 100 kilometers northeast of Warsaw, this former Nazi extermination camp serves as a poignant reminder of the atrocities committed during World War II and the importance of preserving the memory of the victims.

Treblinka was operational from July 1942 to November 1943, during which time an estimated 870,000 to 925,000 Jews were systematically murdered, along with thousands of Roma and Poles. The camp's primary function was to carry out mass extermination, and its facilities were designed with chilling efficiency. Today, the site of Treblinka II, the extermination camp, is marked by a vast field of 17,000 stones, each representing a community whose members were murdered there. The stones, of varying sizes and shapes, stand as a silent tribute to the countless lives lost. A symbolic railway track leads to the camp's entrance, a haunting reminder of the trains that transported victims to their fate.

The memorial also includes a museum that documents the camp's history and operation, showcasing artifacts, photographs, and personal testimonies of survivors. The exhibits offer a chilling glimpse into the unimaginable cruelty and suffering endured by the victims.

A visit to Treblinka is a profoundly moving experience, evoking a range of emotions from grief and anger to disbelief and determination. It is a place that challenges us to confront the darkest chapters of human history and to never forget the victims of this unimaginable tragedy.

**VISITOR INFORMATION**
- **Address:** Treblinka, 08-317 Małkinia Górna
- **Contact:** +48 25 756 53 10
- **Hours:** Open daily, 9:00 AM - 5:00 PM (April-October), 9:00 AM - 4:00 PM (November-March)
- **Admission:** Free
- **Guided Tours:** Available in various languages by prior arrangement.

**TIPS FOR VISITORS**
- **Prepare yourself emotionally:** A visit to Treblinka can be a deeply emotional experience. Take your time, reflect on the history, and remember the victims.
- **Dress respectfully:** Choose attire that is appropriate for a place of remembrance.
- **Maintain silence:** The memorial is a place for quiet contemplation and reflection.
- **Take photos with respect:** While photography is permitted, be mindful of the sensitive nature of the site.

- **VISIT the museum:** The museum provides valuable context and information about the camp's history and operation.
- **Participate in a guided tour:** Guided tours offer deeper insights into the memorial and its significance.

## Żelazowa Wola: Birthplace of Chopin

A pilgrimage for music lovers, Żelazowa Wola beckons with the promise of delving into the world of Frédéric Chopin, Poland's most celebrated composer. Nestled in the heart of Mazovia, a region known for its idyllic landscapes and rich cultural heritage, this charming village is home to the manor house where Chopin was born and spent his early years.

The manor house, a modest yet elegant structure, stands as a testament to the composer's humble beginnings. Step inside and be transported back in time to the early 19th century, as you explore the rooms where Chopin first discovered his passion for music. The house, now a museum, showcases a collection of personal artifacts, musical instruments, and manuscripts that offer a glimpse into the life and creative genius of this iconic figure.

Surrounding the manor house, a serene parkland invites leisurely strolls and quiet contemplation. Lush greenery, vibrant flower beds, and meandering paths create a peaceful oasis where you can imagine the young Chopin finding inspiration amidst the natural beauty.

The heart of Żelazowa Wola's musical legacy lies in the annual Chopin concerts held on the estate grounds. During the summer months, world-renowned pianists grace the stage, their melodies filling the air with the timeless beauty of Chopin's compositions. The concerts, held in an intimate setting against the backdrop of the manor house, offer a unique and moving experience for music lovers of all ages.

## VISITOR INFORMATION
- **Address:** Żelazowa Wola 15, 96-503 Sochaczew
- **Contact:** +48 46 863 33 00
- **Hours** Check the official website for the most up-to-date information.
- **Guided Tours:** Available in various languages.
- **Accessibility:** The manor house and park are partially accessible for visitors with disabilities.

## TIPS FOR VISITORS
- **Check the concert schedule:** If you're interested in attending a Chopin concert, be

sure to check the schedule in advance and book your tickets early.
- **Explore the park:** Take a leisurely stroll through the parkland and discover its hidden corners.
- **Visit the museum:** Learn about Chopin's life and work through the museum's exhibits.
- **Enjoy a meal or a drink:** The estate has a café and restaurant where you can relax and refuel.
- **Purchase souvenirs:** The gift shop offers a variety of Chopin-themed souvenirs.
- 

# Kampinos National Park: Nature Escape

Escape the urban clamor and venture into the wild embrace of Kampinos National Park, a sprawling wilderness just a stone's throw from Warsaw. This UNESCO Biosphere Reserve, a haven of biodiversity, invites you to reconnect with nature and discover the wonders of Poland's unique ecosystems.

Wander through ancient pine forests, where sunlight filters through the canopy, casting dappled shadows on the forest floor. Breathe in the crisp air, scented with pine needles and damp earth, as you listen to the symphony of birdsong. Explore the park's vast network of hiking trails, each revealing a new facet of its natural beauty.

Trek through the marshes and wetlands, where a kaleidoscope of wildflowers blooms in vibrant hues. Observe graceful herons wading through the shallows, or catch a glimpse of a shy beaver building its dam. The park's diverse habitats provide a sanctuary for a wide array of wildlife, from majestic elk to elusive lynx. For a more adventurous experience, rent a bicycle and explore the park's extensive network of cycling routes. Pedal through dense forests, across open meadows, and along sandy dunes, discovering hidden corners and breathtaking vistas at every turn.

Kampinos National Park is not just a playground for nature enthusiasts; it's also a vital protected area, preserving the unique ecosystems of the Mazovian region. Its forests, wetlands, and dunes play a crucial role in maintaining ecological balance, providing a habitat for countless species of plants and animals.

**VISITOR INFORMATION**
- **Address:** Kampinos National Park, Izabelin, Poland
- **Contact:** +48 22 725 50 00
- **Hours:** Open 24 hours
- **Admission:** Free

- **Guided Tours:** Available through the park's visitor center or various tour operators.

**TIPS FOR VISITORS**
- **Plan your route:** The park is vast, so plan your itinerary in advance and choose trails that match your fitness level and interests.
- **Dress appropriately:** Wear comfortable shoes and clothing suitable for outdoor activities.
- **Bring water and snacks:** There are limited facilities within the park, so pack enough supplies for your adventure.
- **Respect the environment:** Stay on designated trails, avoid disturbing wildlife, and pack out all trash.
- **Visit the visitor center:** Learn more about the park's unique ecosystems and conservation efforts.

# CHAPTER 11

## FAQs

Navigating a new city can raise questions, from practical concerns to cultural nuances. To ensure your Warsaw adventure is seamless and enjoyable, we've compiled answers to frequently asked questions, providing you with valuable insights and tips to enhance your travel experience. Whether you're curious about visa requirements, local customs, or the best way to get around, consider this your go-to resource for navigating the intricacies of Warsaw travel. Let's address your queries and equip you with the knowledge you need to embark on your Polish adventure with confidence.

## Your Warsaw Questions Answered
**YOUR WARSAW QUESTIONS ANSWERED**

**Q: Do I need a visa to visit Warsaw?**
A: Visa requirements for Warsaw depend on your nationality and the length of your stay. Citizens of the European Union, the European Economic Area, and several other countries can enter Poland visa-free for up to 90 days within a 180-day period. However,

citizens of certain countries may need to obtain a visa before traveling. It's essential to check the visa requirements for your specific nationality well in advance of your trip.

**Q: What is the best way to get around Warsaw?**
A: Warsaw has an excellent public transportation system, including buses, trams, metro, and suburban trains. Tickets can be purchased at ticket machines or through mobile apps. Taxis and ride-hailing services like Uber and Bolt are also readily available. Cycling is a popular mode of transportation, with numerous bike paths and rental options.

**Q: Is English widely spoken in Warsaw?**
A: While Polish is the official language, English is widely spoken in Warsaw, especially in tourist areas, hotels, restaurants, and shops. However, learning a few basic Polish phrases, such as "dzień dobry" (good morning/day) and "dziękuję" (thank you), will be appreciated by locals.

**Q: What are some cultural customs and etiquette tips I should be aware of?**
A: Poles are generally polite and reserved. It's customary to greet people with a handshake and address them using their title and last name. Avoid being overly loud or boisterous in public. When dining

out, wait to be seated and use utensils to eat, even for pizza.

**Q: Is Warsaw a safe city?**
A: Warsaw is generally a safe city for tourists, but as with any major city, it's important to be aware of your surroundings and take precautions against petty theft. Avoid walking alone in unfamiliar areas at night and keep your valuables secure.

**Q: What is the currency used in Warsaw?**
A: The currency in Poland is the Polish Złoty (PLN). You can exchange currency at banks, exchange bureaus, or withdraw cash from ATMs. Credit cards are widely accepted in hotels, restaurants, and larger shops.

**Q: What are some local customs I should be aware of?**
A: Poles are proud of their heritage and culture. Show respect for their traditions and customs by avoiding sensitive topics, such as politics or religion. Learn a few basic Polish phrases and be open to experiencing the local way of life.

## ADDITIONAL RESOURCES

- **Polish Tourism Organization:** This website provides comprehensive information on

traveling to Poland, including visa requirements, transportation options, and cultural tips.
- **Warsaw Tourist Information Center:** The center offers a variety of resources for visitors, including maps, brochures, and guided tours.
- **Your Embassy or Consulate:** Your embassy or consulate can provide assistance in case of emergencies or lost documents.

*Thank you for purchasing and reading my book. I am extremely grateful and hope you found value in reading it.*

*Please consider sharing it with friends or family and leaving a review online. Your feedback and support are always appreciated, and allows me to continue doing what I love.*

*Please go to the [link](link) if you'd like to leave a review.*

# BONUS

Warsaw, a city of captivating contrasts, offers a myriad of experiences that cater to every traveler's taste and time frame. Whether you have a single day to soak in the highlights or a week to delve deeper into its rich history and vibrant culture, our curated itineraries will help you make the most of your time in the Polish capital.

## One Day in Warsaw: The Essentials

| TIME | ACTIVITY | DESCRIPTION |
|---|---|---|
| Morning | Breakfast at Cafe Bristol | Enjoy a classic European breakfast at the historic Cafe Bristol. |
| Midday | Old Town Square and Royal Castle | Explore the heart of Warsaw's Old Town, visit the Royal Castle. |
| Afternoon | St. John's Archcathedral & Barbican | Visit the Gothic-style cathedral and walk along the historic city walls. |
| Evening | Dinner at Stary Dom Restaurant | Experience traditional Polish cuisine in an elegant setting. |

# Three Days in Warsaw: A Deeper Dive

| DAY | TIME | ACTIVITY | DESCRIPTION |
|---|---|---|---|
| 1 | Full Day | Historical Highlights Tour | Explore Warsaw's Old Town, Royal Castle, and Warsaw Uprising Museum. |
| 2 | Morning | Modern Warsaw | Visit the Palace of Culture and Science, and POLIN Museum. |
|  | Afternoon | Praga District | Discover the bohemian side of Warsaw with street art and the Neon Museum. |
|  | Evening | Dinner and Jazz Club | Enjoy dinner at Falla Warsaw and live jazz at Jazz Club Akwarium. |
| 3 | Morning | Lazienki Park and Palace | Stroll through the park and visit the Palace on the Isle. |

| | | | |
|---|---|---|---|
| | Afternoon | National Museum | Explore a vast collection of art from different periods. |
| | Evening | Dinner at U Fukiera | Experience fine dining at one of Warsaw's oldest restaurants. |

# One Week in Warsaw: The Comprehensive Itinerary

| DAY | TIME | ACTIVITY | DESCRIPTION |
|---|---|---|---|
| 1 | Morning | Breakfast and Old Town Tour | Start with breakfast at Bułkę przez Bibułkę, explore Old Town and Royal Castle. |
| | Afternoon | Warsaw Uprising Museum | Learn about the 1944 Warsaw Uprising. |
| | Evening | Dinner at Stary Dom | Enjoy traditional Polish cuisine. |
| 2 | Morning | Palace of Culture | Visit the observation deck |

|   |           | and Science | for panoramic city views. |
|---|-----------|-------------|--------------------------|
|   | Afternoon | POLIN Museum | Explore the history of Polish Jews. |
|   | Evening   | Praga District and Dinner | Discover Praga District, dinner at Falla Warsaw. |
| 3 | Morning   | Lazienki Park and Palace | Stroll through the park and visit the Palace on the Isle. |
|   | Afternoon | National Museum | Explore a vast collection of art from different periods. |
|   | Evening   | Dinner at U Fukiera | Dine at one of Warsaw's oldest and most prestigious restaurants. |
| 4 | Full Day  | Day Trip to Żelazowa Wola and Kampinos | Visit Chopin's birthplace and enjoy hiking in Kampinos National Park. |
| 5 | Morning   | Breakfast and Copernicus | Start with breakfast at Odette Tea |

| | | Science Centre | Room, explore interactive exhibits. |
|---|---|---|---|
| | Afternoon | Warsaw Zoo | Visit the diverse animal exhibits. |
| | Evening | Chopin Concert in Łazienki Park | Enjoy a live piano concert in the park. |
| 6 | Morning | Tel Aviv Urban Food and Neon Museum | Enjoy breakfast, then explore the Neon Museum. |
| | Afternoon | Shopping at Złote Tarasy | Spend time shopping at this modern mall. |
| | Evening | Dinner at Solec 44 | Experience modern Polish cuisine with a creative twist. |
| 7 | Morning | Breakfast Market and Wilanów Palace | Enjoy breakfast at Warsaw Breakfast Market, visit Wilanów Palace. |
| | Afternoon | Relaxation and Spa at | Treat yourself to a relaxing spa session. |

| | | Hotel Bristol | |
|---|---|---|---|
| | Evening | Final Dinner at Atelier Amaro | Enjoy a Michelin-starred dining experience. |

# HAPPY TRAVEL'S

## From Gregor Steves

Printed in Great Britain
by Amazon